Nathanael West:
A Comprehensive Bibliography

Nathanael West:

A Comprehensive Bibliography

By William White

Oakland University

The Kent State University Press

The Serif Series
Bibliographies and Checklists, Number 32
William White, General Editor
Oakland University

Copyright © 1975 by Kent State University Press
All rights reserved
ISBN 0-87338-157-2
Library of Congress Catalogue Card Number 74-79149
Manufactured in the United States of America
At the Press of The Oberlin Printing Company
Designed by Merald Wrolstad
First Edition

Library of Congress Cataloging in Publication Data

White, William, 1910-
    Nathanael West: a comprehensive bibliography.
    (The Serif series, bibliographies and checklists; no. 32)
    Includes index.
    1. West, Nathanael, 1903-1940—Bibliography.
I. Series.
Z8968.38.W54   016.813'5'2   74-79149
ISBN 0-87338-157-2

Contents

Introduction

Life played dirty tricks on Nathanael West. It may have been collegiate high spirits that account for the comment under his name in the Brown University 1924 year book, "He seems a bit eccentric at times, a characteristic of all geniuses"; but his first novel, *The Dream Life of Balso Snell*, was ignored; the next one, a masterpiece, *Miss Lonelyhearts*, came out just as the publisher was going bankrupt and copies were tied up in litigation; *A Cool Million*'s humor was ill-timed—it was published during the Depression—and the book was remaindered; and *The Day of the Locust* sold only 1,480 copies, prompting West's remark to F. Scott Fitzgerald, "So far the box score stands: Good reviews—fifteen per cent, bad reviews—twenty-five per cent, brutal personal attacks—sixty per cent."

Irony, too, plagued his personal affairs. Although West went to Hollywood after 20th Century Pictures bought *Miss Lonelyhearts*, he never worked on the script and it came out under another title, bearing little resemblance to the original. When he returned to the movie capital his talents were generally wasted on B-pictures, and nine months after he married Eileen McKenney they were both killed in an auto collision near El Centro, California; he was 37 years old.

Ignored alike by readers and critics, except for a few, Nathanael West is not even a name in Alfred Kazin's *On* viii

Native Grounds (New York: Reynal & Hitchcock, 1942),
W. M. Frohock's *The Novel of Violence in America,
1920-1950* (Dallas: Southern Methodist University Press,
1950), Blanche Housman Gelfant's *The American City Novel*
(Norman: University of Oklahoma Press, 1954), or in
Fred B. Millet's *Contemporary American Authors* (New York:
Harcourt, Brace, 1940)—in all of which he deserves a place—
as he does in the first and second editions of James D.
Hart's *Oxford Companion to American Literature* (New York:
Oxford University Press, 1941 and 1948); but he does appear
in the third edition (1956).

New Directions had reprinted *Miss Lonelyhearts* in 1946
and *The Day of the Locust* in 1950; a bare half a dozen
fine essays on his work had appeared, and in May 1957,
The Complete Works of Nathanael West, containing his four
short novels, was published. Just afterwards, my "Nathanael
West: A Bibliography" appeared in *Studies in Bibliography* 11
(1958): 207-224, listing no books on West, one dissertation,
the briefest mention in literary histories, and the few articles
(apart from reviews of the novels)—in a word, his critical
reception was negligible. But as Alexander Pope said:

Ah, for the change 'twixt Now and then!

Not only have all of his novels been reprinted again and
again in numerous editions in both America and England,
but translations have been made into French, German, Italian,
Scandinavian, Portuguese, Polish, Japanese, and other languages.
Further, twelve books and pamphlets have been written
and edited about West and his work, and at least twenty-four
theses and dissertations. No study of 20th century American
literature can now afford to neglect mention of him, as the
material listed below evidences, much of it from my own
previous bibliographies and checklists in *Studies in Bibliography,
The Book Collector, American Book Collector, The Serif,*

and *Bulletin of Bibliography*. All this on a young writer whose total production consisted of four short books, two of which are of uneven quality, and periodical appearances you can count on two hands.

The listing in this bibliography of material by West is chronological, and of material about West is alphabetical by author. Wholly for the benefit and convenience of those working on West, I have included in the appendix his poems, essay, a book review, and his short stories (some revised for use in *Miss Lonelyhearts* and *The Day of the Locust*). Though I hope I have found everything easily available to scholars, critics and librarians, some of it obviously more useful than others, I am sure articles and chapters will have eluded me—I trust not too many of significance.

I am naturally indebted to the editors who published my previous lists, to the bibliographers of *PMLA*, the Modern Humanities Research Association annual bibliographies, the H. W. Wilson guides, *Abstracts of English Studies*, and the other such reference works. Also helpful to me have been Mr. Toby Holtzman, Mr. George A. Masterton, Professor James F. Light, Professor E. R. Hagemann, and especially Professor Jay Martin.

WILLIAM WHITE

Franklin Village, Michigan
20 December 1974

Chronology

A. Books by Nathanael West

1. *The Dream Life of Balso Snell* (1931)

THE DREAM LIFE OF $\frac{\text{BALSO}}{\text{SNELL}}$ / By / N / A / T / H /
A / N / A / E / L / W / E / S / T / CONTACT
EDITIONS / Paris New York / (The title and author
enclosed within rules *rayonnés* in blue, and publisher and
city within vertical rules in black)

Collation: [1]-[98] pp., as follows: [1]-[2] blank; [3]
bastard title: The Dream Life / of / Balso Snell /;
[4] blank; [5] quotation: *"After all, my dear fellow, /
life, Anaxagoras has said, / is a journey." / Bergotte /*;
[6] blank; [7] title-page as above; [8] notices:
Copyright 1931 by / MOSS and KAMIN, Inc. / *Printed
in the United States of States of America.* /; [9]
notice: This edition of "The Dream Life of Balso / Snell"
is limited to 500 numbered copies of / which 300
are for sale in America and 200 for / Great Britain
and the Continent. / This is copy No.   /; [10] blank;
[11] dedication: To A. S. /; [12] blank; 13-95 text:
[96]-[98] blank.

Issued stitched in heavy paper cover folded over paper,
with transparent paper wrapper. Front cover similar to
title-page. Printed in black on spine: THE /D / R / E /
A / M / L / I / F / E / OF / B / A / L / S / O /

S / N / E / L / L / By / N / A / T / H / A / N / A / E / L / W / E / S / T /. All edges untrimmed. The leaves measure 9½ by 6¼ inches.

Published August 1931 in an edition of 500 copies. The original price was $3.00 and (boards) $10.00.

First edition.

Variant bindings:

With a title-page and collation similar to the above, except for the addition of three blank leaves at the back of the book, pp. [99]-[104], copies in "boards," numbered 1 to 15, are actually bound in pale blue and white cloth. Stamped in gold on the front cover: two vertical rules, running from the top to the bottom, with pale blue cloth on the outside and white cloth inside these rules. These rules replace the 8 narrow vertical rules in black on the left, and the 12 narrow vertical rules on the right of the paper-covered edition. The rest of the front cover is similar to the paper covered edition. The matter on the spine is stamped in gold on pale blue cloth instead of being printed in black. The back cover has the same pair of vertical rules in gold, with pale blue cloth on the outside and white cloth inside these rules.

Another copy, in the Holtzman Collection, Birmingham, Michigan, has three extra leaves at the front of the book, pp. [i]-[vi], and is bound in dark blue cloth. The two vertical rules on the front and back covers are narrower than those on the pale blue and white cloth-bound covers. Instead of the matter on the spine of the paper-covered edition and the pale blue and white cloth-bound edition, this dark blue cloth edition's spine has stamped in gold: (heavy rule) / (light rule) / THE / DREAM / LIFE / OF / BALSO / SNELL / BY / WEST / (light rule) / (heavy rule) /.

Still another copy, bound in faded blue cloth over boards, with the same title-page and the same collation as the paper-covered copies, has stamped in black on the spine: (heavy rule) / (light rule) / THE / DREAM / LIFE / OF / BALSO / SNELL / (decoration) / CONTACT / (light rule) / (heavy rule) /. All edges are trimmed. There are two blank leaves at the front, instead of one; there are three blank leaves at the back, instead of one. The leaves measure 9 3/16 by 6 inches, instead of 9½ by 6¼ inches. There is no lettering on the front cover. This copy, now in the Harris Collection, Brown University Library, may be a unique copy, bound by the publishers of Contact Editions (Moss & Kamin, Inc.) as an office copy or for a salesman. (It is numbered 232, the same as my own copy in heavy paper.)

Note: *The Dream Life of Balso Snell* was not reprinted or translated separately but only with *A Cool Million*, or *The Day of the Locust*, or in *The Complete Works*. See descriptions of these books, below, for reprintings.

Excerpts

"The Dear Public." *Americana* 1 (August 1933): 29. (Published in New York City by the Americana Group, Inc., this issue lists Nathaniel [*sic*] West with George Grosz and Gilbert Seldes as Associates on the staff; the editor was Alexander King. West's first name is also misspelled in the by-line.)

"Excerpt." *Americana* 1 (September 1933): 25. (Nathanael West's name is correctly spelled in this issue, and Seldes no longer is on the staff.)

2. *Through the Hole in the Mundane Millstone* (1931)

THE DREAM LIFE OF $\frac{\text{BALSO}}{\text{SNELL}}$ by / Nathanael West (two lines reading downwards) / CONTACT EDITIONS / Paris New York / (The title and author enclosed within rules *rayonnés* and the whole within vertical rules)

Collation: [1]-[4] pp., as follows: [1] title-page on cover as above; [2]-[3] text of "Through the Hole in the / Mundane Millstone" (title at the top of p. [2], with decorated rules at the top and bottom of pp. [2] and [3]); [4] *A Word About* / Contact Editions / (Three Mountains Press) / Paris / (advertisement about Contact Editions on 30 lines, followed by this note: *THE DREAM LIFE OF BALSO SNELL is large octavo, / printed in 14 point Garamond type on CANTERBURY deckle / edge paper. Handsomely bound in de luxe wrappers. The edi- / tion is limited to 500 numbered copies, of which 300 are for / sale in America, and 200 copies for Great Britain and the / Continent.* $3.00 per copy / *There are 15 copies, numbered one to fifteen, bound in Decorated Boards, and signed by the author.* $10.00 per copy/).

Issued as a 4-page leaflet, advertising *The Dream Life of Balso Snell*. The leaves measure 9 7/8 by 7 inches.

Published 1931 not for sale but for private distribution. First edition.

Note: The text of "Through the Hole in the Mundane Millstone" is reprinted in Jay Martin, editor, *Nathanael West: A Collection of Critical Essays*, pp. 29-30, with three variant readings ("Troy; inside" instead of "Troy. Inside" in line 36 of the original; "Lord, a church" instead of "Lord; a church" in line 43; and Kurt Schwitters' definition in italics instead of roman in lines 57-58).

3. *Miss Lonelyhearts* (1933)

(Decorated rule) / (wavy rule) / MISS / LONELY-HEARTS / (short wavy rule) / *by Nathanael West* / (device of monk at writing table) / LIVERIGHT · INC · PUBLISHERS / NEW YORK /

Collation: [1]-[216] pp., as follows: [1] bastard title: MISS LONELYHEARTS /; [2] blank; [3] title-page as above; [4] notices of copyright, printing, and presswork; [5] dedication: TO MAX /; [6] blank; [7]-[8] contents; [9] section half-title [these also occur on pp. 21, 35, 45, 57, 73, 95, 113, 131, 143, 159, 173, 185, 199 and 207, followed by a blank page]; [10] blank; 11-213 text; [214]-[216] blank.

Issued in tan cloth. Stamped on spine in silver on black: (rule) / MISS / LONELYHEARTS / (rule) / NATHANAEL / WEST / (rule) (The above lines enclosed within a silver rule on black) / LIVERIGHT (in silver) /. Top edge yellow; bottom edge trimmed; fore edge untrimmed. The leaves measure 7⅜ by 5 inches.

Published 8 April 1933 in an edition of 2,200 (?) copies. The original price was $2.00.

First edition.

While the first edition was being issued Liveright, Inc. went bankrupt and the printer refused to release 1,400 copies of the book after 800 had been shipped. Publication was finally taken over by Harcourt, Brace and Company, using the plates of the Liveright edition, except for the bottom of the title-page. Replacing the Liveright device was that of Harcourt, Brace, followed by: HARCOURT, BRACE AND COMPANY / NEW YORK /. The verso of the title-page read: COPYRIGHT, 1933, BY NATHANAEL WEST / MANUFACTURED IN THE UNITED STATES OF AMERICA /. The notice of presswork (AT THE VAN REES PRESS) was deleted. Issued in red cloth. Stamped in black on spine: (wavy rule) / *Miss* / *Lonely-* / *hearts* / (wavy rule) / NATHANAEL / WEST / (wavy rule) / *Harcourt*, *Brace* / *and Company* /. Top edge trimmed (not yellow).

Reprintings:

a. (Decorated rule) / (wavy rule) / MISS / LONELY-HEARTS / (short wavy rule) / *by Nathanael West* /

(publisher's device: windmill) / NEW YORK / GREENBERG : PUBLISHER /

213 [3] pp. 1934. 7⅜ by 4⅞ inches. Printed from original plates, with changes, as indicated. Gray cloth. Stamped in blue on front cover: decoration. Stamped in blue on spine: (wavy rule) / *Miss* / *Lonely-* / *hearts* / (wavy rule) / NATHANAEL / WEST / (wavy rule) / (publisher's device: windmill) / GREENBERG /.

b. *Miss* / *Lonelyhearts* / A NOVEL BY / NATHANAEL / WEST / WITH AN / INTRODUCTION / BY ROBERT M. / COATES / *THE NEW CLASSICS* /

[x], 213 [1] pp. New York: New Directions, 24 August 1946 (5,000 copies). 6¾ by 4½ inches. The preliminary pages, pp. [i]-[x], are from new plates, but the text, pp. 11-213, is from the original plates. Red cloth. Stamped in gold on spine, reading downwards: MISS LONELY-HEARTS /. New Classics No. 15. $1.50.

c. *Miss Lonelyhearts* / A NOVEL BY NATHANAEL WEST / With an introduction by Robert M. Coates / THE NEW CLASSICS /

xvi, 142 pp. Second New Classics printing. New York: New Directions, January 1950 (5,000 copies). 7 by 4⅜ inches. Printed entirely from new plates. Yellow cloth. Stamped in black on spine, reading downwards: MISS LONELYHEARTS /. New Classics No. 15. $1.50. A later printing has, opposite the title-page, a longer list of titles (30 instead of 25), in The New Classics Series.

d. Miss Lonelyhearts / NATHANAEL WEST / *Complete and Unabridged* / AVON PUBLICATIONS, INC. / 575 Madison Avenue   New York 22, N. Y. / (The whole across two pages)

95 pp., plus [1] p. of advertisements. 19 April 1955 (190,000 copies). 6⅜ by 4⅛ inches. Paperback. Printed on white front cover: title in white on red, author's name in blue, multicolored illustrations, quotations from reviews in black and red; yellow spine printed in black and red; blurbs on back cover in black and red on gray and yellow. Avon No. 634. 25¢.

e. *Nathanael West* / Miss Lonelyhearts / *Complete and Unabridged* / AVON PUBLICATIONS, INC. / 575 Madison Avenue—New York 22, N.Y. / Copyright, 1933, by Nathanael West. Published by arrange- /ment with New Directions. Introduction, copyright, ©, / 1959, by Avon Publications, Inc. /

96 pp. Second Avon printing: April 1959 (20,000 copies). 6⅜ by 4⅛ inches. The preliminary pages, including the Introduction, pp. ii-iii, and p. 96, are from new plates. Paperback. Printed on black front cover: NATHANAEL WEST (in pink) / T-634 (in white) / Miss (in white) / Lonelyhearts (in white) / With a special introduction by Malcolm Cowley (in white) / (illustration of letter and envelope in red, black, and white) / A savage and reckless novel—(in pink) / "A brilliant and finished (in pink) / piece of writing" –*Edmund Wilson* (in pink) / *An Avon Book—35 cents* (in white) /. Printed on spine, reading downwards: NATHANAEL WEST (pink on white) MISS LONELYHEARTS (white on black) / AVON (in white on black strip in white circle, reading across) / T-634 (in white on black, reading across) /. Printed in white on red back cover, within illustration on newspaper page: blurb for *Miss Lonelyhearts*. Avon No. T-634. 35¢.

The third Avon printing, November 1960 (50,000 copies), and the fourth, November 1962 (25,000 copies)

are similar to the second except in one particular: on the
title-page the name and address of the publisher has
been changed to read, AVON BOOK DIVISION / The
Hearst Corporation / 959 Eighth Avenue /
New York 19, N.Y. /.

f. MISS / LONELYHEARTS / Nathanael West / With
an introduction by / STANLEY EDGAR HYMAN /
An Avon Book / (publisher's device) / (The whole
enclosed within rules curved at the corners)

128 pp. Fifth Avon printing: February 1964 (50,000
copies). 7 3/16 by 4¼ inches. Entirely new plates.
Paperback. Printed in black on front cover: publisher's
device / AVON / GS 1 / 50¢ / NATHANAEL WEST
(in red) / Miss (in script) Lonelyhearts (in script) /
(illustration of heart in black, white, and red) / *"A
COMEDY WITH TRAGIC IMPLICATIONS, /
MISS LONEHEARTS IS A SOLID WORK AS / WELL
AS A BRILLIANT ONE." SATURDAY REVIEW* /
(The whole enclosed within red borders). Printed in
white on red spine, reading downwards: GS1 (reading
across) / *NATHANAEL WEST MISS LONELY-
HEARTS* / (publisher's device) / AVON (reading
across) /. Printed in black on back cover, enclosed within
red borders: blurb for *Miss Lonelyhearts* on 15 lines.
The introduction, taken from Hyman's University
of Minnesota Pamphlet on American Writers, occupies
pp. 5-28; the text, pp. 29-128. West's birth is given as
1902 on p. [1] and as 1903 on p. 5. Avon No. GS 1. 50¢.

The sixth Avon printing, February 1965, contained
the following changes (from the fifth): the line on the
title, "An Avon Book," became "An Avon Library Book";
Hyman's introduction became an afterword and its position

in the book was changed from pp. 5-28 to pp. 105-128;
the pages of the text were thus changed from pp. 29-128
to pp. 5-104; the red borders on the front and back cover
were removed; the red spine became gold, and the
publisher's device was changed to black and moved to
the top, with the bottom of the spine now reading AVON /
GS1 / 50¢ /; and there were other slight changes on the
front and back covers, with the preliminary note on p. [1]
corrected and rewritten.

The seventh (and final) Avon printing, June 1967,
contained a few more changes: the price was raised to
60 cents, the series number was changed from GS1 to SS13,
the outside rounded corners became square, the spine
became red again, the bottom now reading, 13 / AVON /
SS13 / 60¢ /; and the printing data on p. [4] was
brought up to date.

g. MISS / LONELYHEARTS / by / NATHANAEL
WEST / *with an introduction by* / *Alan Ross* / THE
GREY WALLS PRESS / *Crown Passage, Pall Mall* /
London /

116 pp. 1949. 7¼ by 4¾ inches. Blue cloth. Stamped
in silver on spine, reading downwards: *MISS LONELY-
HEARTS* (small heart) *NATHANAEL WEST* / *GREY* /
WALLS / *PRESS* (three lines reading across) /. The
introduction, pp. 7-25, containing a few biographical errors,
is from *Horizon* 18 (October 1948): 284-296; the text
occupies pp. 27-126. 7s 6d.

First British edition.

There is also a variant binding: red-brown cloth instead
of blue, and stamped in black (not silver) on the spine,
reading downwards, MISS LONELYHEARTS
NATHANAEL WEST / GREY / WALLS / PRESS
(three lines reading across) /.

Translations:

h. "Miss Lonelyhearts, aidez-moi, aidez-moi"; "Miss Lonelyhearts en expédition." *L'Arbalète: revue de littérature* (Lyon: Marc Barezat), 9 automne 1944, pp. 193-206.
Translation into French, by Marcelle Sibon, of two chapters from *Miss Lonelyhearts*, "Miss Lonelyhearts, Help Me, Help Me" and "Miss Lonelyhearts on a Field Trip."

i. NATHANAEL WEST / MADEMOISELLE / CŒUR-BRISÉ / "MISS LONELYHEARTS" / *ROMAN* / *Traduit par Marcelle Sibon* / PRÉFACE DE PHILIPPE SOUPAULT / (publisher's device) / ÉDITIONS DU SAGITTAIRE / 56 RUE-RODIER — PARIS / 156 pp. 5 April 1946. 7¼ by 4⅝ inches. Paperback. Printed on front cover: NATHANAEL WEST / LA DEMOISELLE DES / CŒURS BRISÉS / *"MISS LONELYHEARTS"* / ROMAN (in red) / *Traduit par MARCELLE SIBON* / Préface de Philippe Soupault / (drawing of woman's wig, envelopes, and pen) / *D'UNE TERRE A L'AUTRE* (in red) / (eight heavy rules in red) / EDITIONS DU SAGITTAIRE / (two heavy rules in red) /. Printed on spine: NATHANAEL / WEST / La / Demoiselle / des / CŒURES / BRISÉS / SAGITTAIRE /. Printed on back cover in black and red: "Extrait du Catalogue" of Sagittaire. A variant paperback binding has printed on front cover: NATHANAEL WEST / MADEMOISELLE / CŒUR-BRISÉ (in red) / "MISS LONELYHEARTS" / *ROMAN* (in red) / *Traduit par Marcelle Sibon* / PRÉFACE DE PHILLIPE SOUPAULT / (publisher's device in red) / SAGITTAIRE (curved) / (The whole enclosed within red rules, with stars in black at each corner). Printed on spine: NATHANAEL / WEST / Mlle / Cœur- / Brisé / S.P. /

Sagittaire. Printed on back cover in black and red: "Extrait du Catalogue" of Sagittaire (differs from first printing). 125 fr.

Translation into French.

j. SIGNORINA / CUORI-INFRANTI / DI / *Nathanael West* / (flying horse device) / *BOMPIANI* / 144 pp. 1948. 7 by 4⅜ inches. Paperback, with pale blue covers with a broad white stripe. Printed on front cover: SIGNORINA / CUORI-INFRANTI / DI / *West* / PEGASO (flying horse device) LETTERARIO / BOMPIANI /. Printed on spine: *WEST* — SIGNORINA CUORI-INFRANTI (reading upwards) / 10 / (publisher's device) /. Printed on back cover: Lire trecento / 7463 / N /. Translated by Bruno Maffi. Published by Valentino Bompiani & C., Milano, Firenze, Roma. Pegaso Letterario No. 10. L. 300.

Translation into Italian.

k. [In Japanese characters:] Kodoku-na Musume / N. West / Translated by S. M. 212 pp. 15 June 1955. 6¾ by 4 inches. Paperback. Translated by Saiichi Maruyama. Published by Naomichi Tōyama, Dabiddo-sha (David Company, Ltd.), Tokyo. ¥ 120.

Translation into Japanese.

l. NATHANAEL WEST / *Fru Hjärtesorg* / Rabén & Sjögren / Vi / 104 pp. 1955. 6 11/16 by 4 1/16 inches. Papercovered boards, with an orange and purple design and printing on front cover (Nathanael West / Fru Hjärtsorg /), spine, and back cover. Printed on spine, reading downwards: NATHANAEL WEST / *Fru Hjärtesorg* / 4 (reading

across) /. Translated by Anna Rapp. Partisan-serien No. 4.
Kr. 7:50.

Translation into Swedish.

m. NATHANAEL WEST / Schreiben Sie / Miss Lonely-
hearts / EIN ROMAN / INS DEUTSCHE ÜBER-
TRAGEN / VON FRITZ GÜTTINGER / MIT EINER
EINFÜHRUNG / VON ALAN ROSS / DIOGENES
VERLAG ZÜRICH /

138 pp., plus 5 [1] pp. of advertisements. 1961.
7⅛ by 4¼ inches. Purple cloth. Stamped in white
on spine, reading upwards: WEST Miss Lonelyhearts /.
Foreword, pp. 5-10 from Alan Ross's Introduction to
West's *Complete Works*. 12.80 D.M.

Translation into German.

n. NATHANAEL WEST / Schreiben Sie / Miss Lonelyhearts / EIN ROMAN / MIT EINER EINFÜHRUNG /
VON ALAN ROSS / FISCHER BÜCHEREI /

142 pp., plus 2 pp. of advertisements. June 1963.
7⅛ by 4 3/16 inches. Paperback with illustrations on
front cover, spine, and back cover in red, blue, and black.
The text and introduction are the same as the Diogenes
edition above, but the book has been completely reset.

Translation into German.

o. Nathanael West / *Schreiben Sie* / *Miss Lonelyhearts* /
Roman / *Aus dem Amerikanischen von* / *Fritz*
Güttinger / *Mit einer Einführung von* / *Alan Ross* /
Diogenes

138 pp. Zurich, 1972. 7 by 4⅛ inches. Paperback.
Printed on front cover: Nathanael / West / (dot in gray) /
Schreiben Sie / Miss / Lonelyhearts / *Roman* / (drawing of
typewriter and flag, with red stripes) / Diogenes / (The
whole enclosed within rules in gray). Printed on back cover:

note on West and the novel. Printed on spine, reading
upwards: • detebe 40/I Nathanael West (large dot in gray)
Schreiben Sie Miss Lonelyhearts /.

Translation into German.

The text and introduction are printed from plates of the
Diogenes 1961 clothbound edition; pp. [1], [3] and [4],
containing the bastard title, title page and verso, have been reset;
the advertisements at the back have been dropped. This printing
appears as Diogenes Taschenbuch 40/I, a companion volume to
Tag der Heuschrecke, Diogenes Taschenbuch 40/II.

p. [In Arabic characters:] Nathanael West / Del-šekaste /
Translated by Abdollāh Tavakkol / (publisher's
device) /

200 pp. Tehran: Morvārid, 1962. 6½ by 4⅜ inches.
Paperback, with multicolored illustration, author, title,
publisher, translator on front cover in white on red,
red and blue on white; in white on red spine, reading
upwards; and blurb in blue on white on back cover, with
broad red vertical strip. Introduction, pp. 5-11, by translator.
I am indebted to the American Embassy in Tehran
for sending me a copy.

Translation into Iranian (Persian).

q. NATHANAEL WEST / FRU / HJERTESORG /
På dansk ved / HANS HERTEL / ARENA.
Fredensborg 1962 /

156 pp. 8¼ x 5¼ inches. Paperback, with newspaper
drawing, author and title on front cover in tan, black,
red, and white. Printed in black and red on spine,
reading downwards: NATHANAEL WEST: FRU
HJERTESORG /. Blurb in black on back cover.
D. kr. 18,75.

Translation into Danish.

r. NATHANAEL WEST / *Frøken Hjertesukk* / OVER-
SATT AV / GUNNEL MALMSTRÖM / FORLAGT
AV / H. ASCHEHOUG & CO. (W. NYGAARD) /
OSLO 1965 /

113 [3] pp. 7¾ x 4⅝ inches. Rough pale grey cloth.
Stamped in gold on front cover: heart design. Lettered
in black on spine, reading downwards: NATHANAEL
WEST · FRØKEN HJERTESUKK /. Foreword, pp. 5-10,
translated from Alan Ross's Introduction to West's
Complete Works. N. kr. 15,50 (paper), 22,50 (cloth).
Translation into Norwegian.

s. Nathanael West / Vastaathan kirjeeseeni / Miss
Lonelyhearts / Suomentanut / ANTERO TIUSANEN /
Amerikkalainen alkuteos / MISS LONELYHEARTS /
© by Nathanael West 1933 / WERNER SÖDER-
STRÖM OSAKEYHTIÖ-PORVOO · HELSINKI /
(The whole across two pages)

117 [1] pp., plus 5 [1] pp. of advertisements. 1966.
7¾ x 4¾ inches. Black cloth. Stamped in blind on front
cover: large letter a within rules; lettered in white: west /
vastaathan kirjeeseeni, / Miss Lonelyhearts /. Lettered
in white on spine, reading downwards; west a (on
green background, reading across) Miss Lonelyhearts /.
Introduction, pp. [7]-[12], by the translator.
Translation into Finnish.

Original Appearances:

t. "Miss Lonelyhearts and the Lamb." *Contact* 1 (February
1932): 80-85. (This chapter and the others below
are early versions of chapters 3, 2, 5, 8 and 7, with
considerable variation; they are listed below under "Work
Originally Published in Periodicals" and reprinted
in Appendix, below. See also Carter A. Daniel, "West's

Revisions of *Miss Lonelyhearts*," *Studies in Bibliography*
16 [1963]: 232-243.)

u. "Two Chapters from Miss Lonelyhearts: Miss Lonelyhearts
and the Dead Pan [and] Miss Lonelyhearts and the
Clean Old Man." *Contact* 1 (May 1932): 13-21, 22-27.

v. "Miss Lonelyhearts in the Dismal Swamp."
Contempo 2 (5 July 1932): 1, 2.

w. "Miss Lonelyhearts on a Field Trip." *Contact* 1
(October 1932): 50-57.

4. *A Cool Million* (1934)

A COOL / MILLION /. *The Dismantling of Lemuel Pitkin* /
BY / NATHANAEL WEST / (ornament) /
COVICI · FRIEDE · *Publishers* / NEW YORK /

Collation: [1]-[236] pp., as follows: [1] bastard title:
A COOL MILLION /; [2] blank; [3] title-page
as above; [4] notices of copyright, reservation of rights,
printing, press-work, and designer; [5] dedication:
TO / S. J. PERELMAN /; [6] blank; [7] half title:
A COOL MILLION / ; [8] quotation: *"John D.
Rockefeller would give a cool million / to have a
stomach like yours."*—OLD SAYING /; 9-229 text;
[230]-[236] blank.

Issued in light tan cloth. Stamped in green on front cover:
A COOL / MILLION / (ornament) /. Stamped in green
on spine: WEST / A COOL MILLION (reading
downwards) / *Covici · Friede* /. Top edge yellow; fore
and bottom edges trimmed. The leaves measure
7⅜ by 5 inches.

Published 19 June 1934 in an edition of 3,000 (?) copies.
The original price was $2.00.

First edition.

A variant binding has turned up, bound in green cloth, stamped in black on the front cover and on the spine; the top edge is trimmed but is not yellow; and instead of the imprint at the base of the spine, *Covici · Friede*, there is a rule across the spine. Copies are in the collection of Mr. Allan Covici, University of California reference librarian and proprietor of the Invisible Bookshop of Berkeley, and the Holtzman Collection, Birmingham, Michigan. Another copy, similar to Mr. Covici's, is in the Holtzman Collection, Birmingham, and also in my own collection; but this one is bound in rust-colored cloth.

The dust jacket contains this biographical sketch:

Born in New York City, 1904.

Attended local high schools and then preparatory school in New England.

Graduated from Brown University in 1924.

Worked as a construction superintendent and then went to Paris 1926-28. While there wrote "The Dream Life of Balso Snell," a novelette which was published in 1931 by Contact Editions.

With W. C. Williams and Robert McAlmon edited a quarterly literary review called "Contact." This was after his return from Paris.

Again in the construction business, but changed to hotel management. For a time he operated a skyscraper hotel in the East Side of New York City.

In the Spring of 1933 his novel, "Miss Lonelyhearts," was published, causing a furor among critics who hailed the arrival of an important figure in the literary world.

Went Hollywood, but only for a Summer.

Now lives on a farm in Pennsylvania, and spends most of his time writing. Manages, however, to do a bit of hunting and run dogs in field trials.

"A Cool Million" was written without malice.

Most likely written by West—or at least supplied by him—the information is at variance with the known facts: he was not born in 1904, he attended no preparatory school in New England, he was not in Paris 1926-28 (but less than three months in October 1926-January 1927), and *Miss Lonelyhearts* hardly "caused a furor among critics" in 1933. The novelist's humor and bent for fantasy were working overtime here.

Reprintings:

a. A COOL / MILLION / Nathanael West / (publisher's device) / A BERKLEY MEDALLION BOOK / published by / THE BERKLEY PUBLISHING CORPORATION /

[ii], 142 pp. June 1961, 100,000 copies. 7 1/16 by 4 3/16 inches. Paperback with author, title, price and illustration on front cover in blue, black, and gold; lettering on spine and back cover in blue and black. Berkley Medallion No. BG537. 50¢.

b. *Two Novels by* / NATH / ANAEL / WEST / *The Dream Life of Balso Snell* / *A Cool Million* / Noonday Press / a division of / Farrar, Straus and Company: New York / (Title covers two pages, with author's name on three uneven lines)

[viii], 184 pp. 7 March 1963, 6,000 copies. 8 by 5⅜ inches. Paperback with illustration on front cover in black, green, and blue; lettering on spine in black, green, and blue; lettering on back cover in white on blue. Noonday No. N244. $1.65. The text is printed from plates of the two novels in the Farrar, Straus edition of *The Complete Works of Nathanael West*.

Second printing, 1965, with the only change the insertion of the line, "Second Printing 1965," under "First Noonday Press Printing, 1963," on p. [iv]. Third printing, 1967, adds another line, "Third printing, 1967," on p. [iv]. Fourth printing, 1969, adds another line, *"Fourth printing, 1969,"* on p. [iv], and a line has been added

at the top of the back cover, "N 244—Literature";
also the address of the publisher at the bottom of the
back cover has been changed from New York 3 to New York
10003. By the eighth printing, 1973, the price had been
raised to $1.95 (changed on the front and back covers),
dates of other printings no longer noted on p. [iv], which
now has "*Eighth printing, 1973*" under the line, "All
rights reserved"; at the top of the back cover has been
added the number, "SBN 374.5.0292.7."

c. A COOL MILLION / THE DREAM LIFE / OF BALSO
   SNELL / Nathanael West / An Avon Library Book /
   (publisher's device) / (The whole enclosed within
   rules, rounded at the corners)

158 [2] pp. April 1965. 7⅛ x 4⅛ inches, rounded at
the outside corners. Paperback, with red and black lettering
on front and back covers, and a multicolored illustration
on front cover. Lettered on spine: (publisher's device) /
NATHANAEL WEST (in red, reading downwards) /
A COOL MILLION and (reading downwards) / THE
DREAM LIFE OF BALSO SNELL (reading downwards) /
AVON / SS6 / 60¢ /.

Second printing, March 1969, has several changes:
the outside corners of the covers are no longer rounded;
the front and back covers and the spine are slightly
redesigned (though the drawing of Lemuel Pitkin has
been retained); the Avon Library No. has been changed to
NS39; the price raised to 95¢; the biographical matter
on p. [1] rewritten; publishing details on p. [4] have been
reset and the line, "Second Printing, March, 1969,"
added; p. [159] is blank, and the Avon Library
advertisement on p. [160] entirely rewritten.

Third printing, May 1973, has further changes: the
front and back covers and the spine have been entirely
redesigned (with a wholly new multicolored drawing);
the title-page reads: A COOL MILLION / THE DREAM
LIFE / OF BALSO SNELL / NATHANAEL WEST /
(publisher's device) BARD BOOKS / PUBLISHED
BY AVON / (The whole enclosed within rules, rounded
at the corners); p. [4] has been reset and the line,
"Third Printing, May, 1973," substituted for the line
about the second printing; the Bard Avon No. 15115
appears at the top of the front cover and the new, raised,
price of $1.65; both pages [159] and [160] contain ad-
vertisements for Bard Books.

d. A COOL / MILLION / *The Dismantling of Lemuel
Pitkin* / BY / NATHANAEL WEST / (ornament) /
(publisher's device: lion and spear) / NEVILLE
SPEARMAN / *London* / (The whole enclosed within
a rule within decorated rules)

139 [1] pp. 1954. 7¼ by 4⅞ inches. Stamped in white
on spine: A / COOL / MILLION / (decorated rule) /
Nathanael / West / (publisher's device: lion and spear) /
NEVILLE / SPEARMAN /. 9s. 6d.
First British edition.

e. NATHANAEL WEST / (two thin rules) / MISS
LONELYHEARTS / AND / A COOL MILLION /
PENGUIN BOOKS /

176 pp. Harmondsworth, Middlesex, 1961. 7 3/16 by
4 5/16 inches. Paperback with illustration on front cover
in black, lettering in black on gray, and publisher's device
in black on orange; similar lettering on spine and back cover.
Penguin Modern Classics No. 1567. 2s. 6d. A note on
p. [1] says, in error, that West "lived in Paris from 1924

to 1931, and there published his first novel." He was
back in New York by 1927, and *Balso Snell* was printed in
New York, although Paris is also given as the place of
publication. P. [4] further errs in giving Secker & Warburg
in 1957 as first English publishers of *Miss Lonelyhearts*
and *A Cool Million*; the former was first published in
England by Grey Walls Press, 1949, and the latter
by Neville Spearman, 1954.

Reprinted in 1966. Paperback cover has been redesigned,
with the publisher's device (penguin) in orange and
black, titles in orange and black, and the spine and back
cover in orange with white and black lettering. 3*s.* 6*d.*
There are some slight changes on p. [1] but the errors
are retained; the errors on p. [4] have been corrected
and the page reset. On the title-page, the publisher's device
(penguin) has been inserted above the line PENGUIN
BOOKS.

Translation:

f. *En kall miljon*. Translated by Thomas Warburton.
   Stockholm: Gerber, 1970. 132 pp. 13:50.
   Translation into Swedish. Not seen.

5. *The Day of the Locust* (1939)

   Nathanael West / THE DAY / OF THE / LOCUST /
   Random House, New York / (Half-inch right-angle
   rules at each corner)

   Collation: [i]-[viii] + [1]-[240] pp.,as follows: [i]-[ii]
   blank: [iii] publisher's device: house; [iv] note:
   Other Books by / Nathanael West: / Miss Lonelyhearts / A Cool Million /; [v] title-page as above;
   [vi] notices: Copyright, 1939, by / Random House,
   Inc. / First Printing / Manufactured in / the U.S.A.

by / H. Wolff, New York /; [vii] dedication: For Laura /; [viii] blank; [1] half title: The Day of the Locust /; [2] blank; 3-238 text; [239]-[240] blank.

Issued in red cloth. Orange paper label on spine, lettered: West / THE DAY / OF THE / LOCUST / Random / House / (3/16-inch right-angle rules at each corner). Top edge black; fore and bottom edges trimmed. The leaves measure 8 by 5 inches. Published 16 May 1939 in an edition of 3,000 copies. The original price was $2.00.

First edition.

Note: Line 6, p. 115, first word reads "thought" instead of "though."

Reprintings:

a. NATHANAEL WEST / *The Day of the Locust* / WITH AN INTRODUCTION BY RICHARD B. GEHMAN / THE NEW CLASSICS /

xxiv, 167 [1] pp. New York: New Directions, 28 August and December 1950 (5,000 copies each printing). 7 by 4¾ inches. Light green cloth. Stamped in black on spine, reading downwards: THE DAY OF THE LOCUST /. New Classics No. 29. $1.50.

b. THE DAY OF THE / LOCUST / WITH AN INTRO-DUCTION BY / RICHARD B. GEHMAN / by NATHANAEL WEST / (publisher's device: bantam) BANTAM BOOKS • *New York* / (2¾-inch vertical decorated rule above publisher's device)

xvi, 144 pp. March 1953 (250,000 copies). 6⅜ by 4¼ inches. Paperback with multicolored illustration on front cover. Spine and back cover in yellow, blue, red, and black. Bantam No. 1093. 25¢

c. THE / DAY / OF / THE / LOCUST / *With an Intro-duction by / Richard B. Gehman* / by / Nathanael West / Bantam Books (publisher's device) New York / xx, 140 pp. December 1957. Second Bantam printing (new edition). 7 by 4⅛ inches. Paperback with multicolored illustration on front cover. Lettering on spine in white on black with red publisher's device; lettering on back cover in black, purple, and red with yellow and red illustration. Bantam No. A1704. 35¢.

d. THE DAY / OF THE LOCUST / by / NATHANAEL WEST / *With an Introduction by* / RICHARD B. GEHMAN / (decoration) / BANTAM BOOKS / NEW YORK /

xx, 140 pp. January 1959. Third Bantam printing. 7 by 4⅛ inches. Black paperback cover with a multicolored illustration and lettering in white; lettering on spine in gold and back cover in white. With the exception of the preliminary pages, pp. [i],[ii],[iv], the title-page, and p. 140, and the cover, this printing is similar to the second Bantam printing. But the book has now become a Bantam Classic, No. AC14.

With the fourth printing, July 1960, the number was changed to FC144, the spine lettering is in white, and the price raised to 50¢. Otherwise, it is similar to the third printing. The fifth printing, October 1961; sixth printing, January 1963—only the cover was somewhat changed (still black), and a new number FC184. On the seventh printing, October 1964, there was a new number again, SC272, and a further increase in price to 75¢. The publishing figure available from Bantam Books, Inc. was that their "total printings thus far approximate 475,000 units". Sidney B. Kramer, Senior Vice President, also said, "The behavior of Nathanael West's *Day of the Locust* in terms of reader interest is very high. Not many books

have enough demand to keep them constantly in print."
The title-page of the seventh and eighth Bantam printings
reads: THE DAY / OF THE LOCUST / by /
NATHANAEL WEST / WITH AN INTRODUCTION
BY / RICHARD B. GEHMAN / (decoration) /
BANTAM BOOKS / (rule) / NEW YORK /
TORONTO / LONDON /. The price of the eighth
printing (1966) (indicated on the front cover and
spine) was 95¢. The introduction and text of all the
Bantam printings from the third to the eighth are identical.

e. Nathanael West / (line of hearts) / Miss Lonelyhearts /
& / The Day of the / Locust / (line of hearts) /
A New Directions Paperbook /

viii, 248 pp. October 1962, 10,000 copies; November
1963 (second printing), 10,000 copies. 7⅛ by 4 3/16
inches. Paperback, with a photographic design in black
on gray front cover; white lettering on black on spine,
reading downwards: West Miss Lonelyhearts & The Day
of the Locust ND PAPERBOOK 125 /; black lettering
on white back cover. $1.60. The text of *The Day of
the Locust*, pp. 1-167, is from plates of New Direction's
New Classics edition, 1950, with Richard B. Gehman's
introduction; the text of *Miss Lonelyhearts*, pp. 169-247,
is a new setting. A brief biographical note is on pp. v-vi.
The differences between the first and second printings
of the New Directions Paperbook occur inside the front
cover, on pp. [iv] and [248], and inside the back cover.
The legend "SECOND PRINTING" is also on the
back cover.

The third through the sixth printings of this edition
are identical with the second printing except for p. [iv]
and the legends at the top of the back cover, THIRD

PRINTING, FOURTH PRINTING, FIFTH PRINTING, and SIXTH PRINTING; the advertisement of New Directions Paperbooks on p. [248] is missing in the sixth printing.

f. Nathanael West / (line of hearts) / Miss Lonelyhearts / & / The Day of the / Locust / (line of hearts) / A New Directions Paperbook /

[vi], 185 [1] pp. 1969. 8 by 5⅜ inches. Paperback, with photographic design in black on gray front cover; white lettering on black on spine, reading downwards: West Miss Loneyhearts & The Day of the Locust NDP125 /; black lettering on white back cover (blurbs about the two novels and West, and a quotation from F. Scott Fitzgerald). $1.75. *Miss Lonelyhearts*, pp. 1-58; and *The Day of the Locust*, pp. 59-185, have been entirely reset from earlier New Directions printings; no introduction, no advertisements; they are numbered the seventh through eleventh printings and are identical except for the legends on p. [iv] and at the top of the back cover: SEVENTH PRINTING, EIGHTH PRINTING, NINTH PRINTING, TENTH PRINTING, and ELEVENTH PRINTING; the tenth and eleventh printings also have eight comments on the two novels on p. [ii]. The eleventh printing has the ISBN on back cover. The total number of copies printed in all eleven printings (through April 1974) is 389,000.

g. THE / *day* / OF THE / *locust* / *NATHANAEL WEST* / *With* / *a new* / *introduction* / *by* / *Budd Schulberg* / (publisher's device) / TIME READING PROGRAM SPECIAL EDITION / TIME INCORPORATED · NEW YORK /

xxiv, 167 [1] pp. 1965. / 8 x 5¼ inches. Flexible plastic cover. Lettered on front cover: NATHANAEL (in pink) / WEST (in pink) / The Day (in white) / of (in white) / the Locust (in white) /. Front and back covers and spine: multicolored montage illustration. Lettered on spine, reading downwards: NATHANAEL WEST The Day of the Locust TIME INC. / (Author's name in pink, title and publisher in white). Issued as a title in *Time Magazine's* Reading Program, by subscription; individual titles not for sale. The Editor's Preface (by The Editors of Time) occurs on pp. vii-xii, and Schulberg's Introduction on pp. xiii-xxiii.

h. THE DAY / OF THE LOCUST / BY NATHANAEL WEST / THE GREY WALLS PRESS / CROWN PASSAGE, PALL MALL / LONDON S. W. 1 /

208 pp. 1951. 7¼ by 4¾ inches. Dark blue cloth. Stamped in gold on spine, reading downwards: *Nathanael West* THE DAY OF THE LOCUST /; reading across: GREY / WALLS / PRESS /. 9s. 6d.

First British edition.

i. NATHANAEL WEST / THE DAY OF THE LOCUST / (short rule) / THE DREAM LIFE OF / BALSO SNELL / PENGUIN BOOKS / IN ASSOCIATION WITH / SECKER & WARBURG /

215 [1] pp., plus [8] pp. of advertisements. Harmondsworth, Middlesex, 1963. 7⅛ by 4¼ inches. Orange paperback. Lettered in black on front cover: (publisher's device on white) a Penguin Book 4'- / (rule) / The Day of the / Locust / (rule) / Nathanael West / (large illustration of a face in black and white and brown) /. Lettered in black on spine, reading downwards: Nathanael West (in white) The Day of the Locust / (publisher's device on white) / 1884 (reading across) /. Lettered in black on back cover: (publisher's device on white) a

Penguin Book / (rule) / The Day of the / Locust / (16-line description of *The Day of the Locust* and 3-line description of *The Dream Life of Balso Snell*) / *For copyright reasons this edition is not for sale in the U.S.A. or Canada /*. Penguin Books No. 1884. 4s. A note on p. [4] says, "Both were first published in Great Britain by Secker & Warburg 1957." This is not accurate: *The Day of the Locust* was first published by the Grey Walls Press in 1951. Although this is a printing of two novels, the front cover and the spine refer only to *The Day of the Locust*.

Translations:

j. *Il giorno della locusta*. Translated by Carlo Fruttero. Torino: Einaudi, 1952. 224 pp. L. 1000.
Translation into Italian. Not seen.

k. NATHANAEL WEST / GRÄSHOPPORNA / Översättning och förord / av / REIDER EKNER / (publisher's device) / CHRISTOFERS BOKFÖRLAG / STOCKHOLM /
201 [3] pp. 1959. 7⅞ by 5⅜ inches. Paperback. Printed on orange front cover: (Drawing in black on white strip of movie film) / GRÄS- (in purple) / HOPPORNA (in purple) / NATHANAEL (in purple) / WEST (in purple) /. Printed in black on spine, reading downwards: *Nathanael West* (dot) GRÄSHOPPORNA /. Blurb in black on back cover. Introduction, pp. 5-14, by the translator. 14:50, inb. 18:—.
Translation into Swedish.

l. NATHANAEL WEST / IL GIORNO / DELLA LOCUSTA / Traduzione di Carlo Fruttero / (publisher's device) / ARNOLDO MONDADORI EDITORE /
176 pp. Milano: 1960. 7⅞ by 5¼ inches. Heavy paperback cover, with red cloth backstrip. Printed in black on green front cover: NATHANAEL WEST (in white) /

IL GIORNO / DELLA LOCUSTA / ARNOLDO / MONDADORI / EDITORE / LIRE 600 / (illustration in black, red, and white) /. Printed in black on spine, reading upwards, 64 / Nathanael West-IL GIORNO DELLA LOCUSTA / M (ornamental letter) /. Printed in black on back cover: biographical sketch and photograph of Nathanael West. Il Bosco, Vol. 64. L. 600.

Translation into Italian.
The text is the same as the Einaudi edition above, but the book has been completely reset. Opposite the title-page, the author, title, and translator are repeated in similar type, but the publisher's device and name differ: GIULIO EINAUDI EDITORE /.

m. COLECÇÃO MINIATURA / *NATHANAEL WEST* / A PRAGA DOS (in red) / GAFANHOTOS (in red) / *Tradução de* / ALFREDO MARGARIDO / (publisher's device) / EDICÃO 'LIVROS DO BRASIL' LISBOA / (The whole inclosed within three rules in red)

179 [5] pp. 1961. 6 5/16 by 4⅛ inches. Pale green paperback. Printed on front cover: *NATHANAEL WEST* (in black) / A PRAGA (in red) / DOS GAFANHOTOS (in red) / multicolored drawing in circle of movie "types") / COLECÇÃO (dot) MINIATURA (in white) / EDICAO "LIVROS DO BRASIL" LISBOA / (The whole over white rules). Printed on spine, reading upwards: COLECÇÃO / MINIATURA (in black) / A PRAGA DOS GAFANHOTOS (in red) / NATHANAEL / WEST (in black) /. 128 (reading across) /. Printed in black and red on back cover: blurb for Colecção Miniatura.

Translation into Portuguese.

n. NATHANAEL WEST / DZIEŃ (in red) / SZAR-AŃCZY (in red) / (star in red) / MISS (in red) /

28

LONELYHEARTS (in red) / *tłumaczła* / *Maria Skibniewska* / 1963 / CZYTELNIK / 352 pp. 5⅞ x 4⅛ inches. Red cloth. Stamped in black on front cover: animal device. Stamped in black on spine: N. WEST / DZIEŃ / SZARAŃCZY / (rule) / MISS / LONELYHEARTS / CZYTELNIK /. Cena ZŁ 18.—.
Translation into Polish of *Miss Lonelyhearts* and *The Day of the Locust*.

o. *Juffrouw Hartzeer. De achtste plaag.* Translated by Cees Boos. Amsterdam: Arbeiderspers, 1967. 269 pp. Fl. 8.50.
Translation into Dutch of *Miss Lonelyhearts* and *The Day of the Locust*. Not seen.

p. *Požár Hollywoodu.* Translated by Jaroslav Schejbal. Praha: Mladá Fronta, 1968. 330 pp. 15 Kčs.
Translation into Slavic. Not seen.

q. NATHANAEL WEST / Tag der / Heuschrecke / EIN ROMAN / INS DEUTSCHE ÜBERTRAGEN / VON FRITZ GÜTTINGER / DIOGENES VERLAG /. 256 pp. 7⅛ x 4⅛ inches. Zurich, 1964. Black cloth. Lettered in gold on red on spine: NATHANAEL / WEST / (rule) / *Tag der* / *Heuschrecke* /. Sw. fr. 10, 80.
Translation into German.
Reprinted in paperback by Fischer Bücherei, Frankfurt am Main, 1968, 154 pp., D.M. 2.80. Not seen.

r. Nathanael West / *Tag der Heuschrecke* / *Roman* / *Aus dem Amerikanischen* / *von Fritz Güttinger* / Diogenes / 256 pp. Zurich, 1972. 7 by 4⅛ inches. Paperback. Printed on front cover: Nathanael / West / (dot in gray) / Tag der / Heuschrecke / *Roman* / (drawing of woman riding a skeleton of a horse, with a red cap) / Diogenes /. (The whole enclosed within rules in gray). Printed on back cover: note on West and the novel. Printed on spine, reading upwards: : detebe 40/II Nathanael West (large dot in gray) Tag der Heuschrecke /.

Translation into German.

The text is printed from the plates of the Diogenes 1964 clothbound edition; pp. [1], [3] and [4], containing the bastard title, title page and verso, have been reset. This printing appears as Diogenes Taschenbuch 40/II, a companion volume to *Schreiben Sie Miss Lonelyhearts,* Diogenes Taschenbuch 40/I.

s. *Inago no hi.* Translated by Itakura Akira. Tokyo: Kadokawa Shoten, 1970. 288 pp. ¥200.

Translation into Japanese. Not seen.

t. Nathanael West / Il giorno della locusta / Traduzione di Carlo Fruttero / Einaudi /

[iv], 210 [6] pp. Torino, 1973. 7⅝ by 4½ inches. Paperbound. Printed on front cover: Nathanael West / Il giorno della locusta / (drawing in color by Edward Hopper of a man and a woman, with a waiter, at a lunch counter, enclosed within rules in red within rules in blue) / Einaudi /. Printed on back cover: note on West and the novel. Printed on spine, reading downwards: West Il giorno della locusta / (publisher's device, reading across) / 68 (reading across) /. The 68 refers to the series number: Nuovi Coralli 68. Lire 1400.

Translation into Italian.

The text is the same as the other Einaudi editions, but the book has been completely reset.

u. *Saskajárás.* Translated by Vera Vándor. Budapest: Magvető Kiadó, 1971. 212 pp. 23.-Ft.

Translation into Hungarian. Not seen.

v. *Saskajárás.* Translated by Vera Vándor. Bratislava: Madách Konyvkiadó, 1971. 212 pp. 18 Kčs.

Translation into Czech (Magyar). Not seen. May be the same as translation above.

Original Appearance:

w. "Bird and Bottle." *Pacific Weekly* 5 (10 November 1936): 329-331. (This chapter is an early version of Chapter 14, with considerable variation; it is listed below under "Work Originally Published in Periodicals" and reprinted in Appendix, below.)

6. *The Complete Works* (1957)

The Complete Works of / NATH / ANAEL / WEST / Farrar, Straus and Cudahy : New York / (Title covers two pages, with author's name on three uneven lines)

Collation: [i]-[ii] + [i]-xxii + [1]-[424] pp., as follows: [i]-[ii] blank; [i] blank; [ii]-[iii] title-page as above; [iv] notices: © 1957 by Farrar, Straus & Cudahy, Inc. / Copyright 1931 by Moss and Kamin / Copyright 1933, 1934 by Nathanael West / Copyright 1939 by the estate of Nathanael West / Library of Congress catalog card number 57-6259 / Manufactured in the United States of America / by H. Wolff, New York / First printing, 1957 / Design: MARSHALL LEE /; [iv]-[v] contents; [vi] blank; [vii]-xxii "The Dead Center: An Introduction to Nathanael West," by Alan Ross; [1] half title: *1931* / *The Dream Life of Balso Snell* /; [2] dedication and quotation: To A. S. / *"After all, my dear fellow, / life, Anaxagoras has said, / is a journey."* / BERGOTTE /; [3]-62 text; [63] half title: *1933* / *Miss Lonelyhearts* /; [64] dedication: To MAX /; [65]-140 text; [141] half title: *1934* / A *Cool Million* / or, The Dismantling of Lemuel Pitkin /; [142] dedication and quotation: To S. J. PERELMAN / *"John D. Rockefeller would give a cool million to have a stomach / like yours."*—OLD SAYING /; [143]-255 text; [256] blank; [257] half title: *1939* /*The Day*

of the Locust /; [258] dedication: For LAURA /;
[259]-421 text; [422]-[424] blank.

Issued in black paper-covered boards with a yellow
cloth backstrip. Stamped in blind on front cover: NATH /
ANAEL / WEST / (Uneven lines, as on title-page).
Stamped in white on spine: *The* / *Complete Works* / *of* /
Nathanael / *West* / Farrar, Straus & Cudahy / (Initial
letter of author's last name in black). Top edge black;
fore and bottom edges trimmed. The leaves measure
7¼ by 5 inches.

Published 10 May 1957 in an edition of 7,600 copies.
The original price was $5.00.

First edition.

Note: An errata slip is inserted, loose, in the book, calling
attention to errors in the introduction. The year of his birth is
given, p. x, as 1906; the errata slip gives it as 1903; his age is
given, p. x, as thirty-four when he died; the errata slip gives it as
thirty-seven. The introduction mentions that he was associate
editor of *Americana* (with George Grosz); the errata slip says that
he was associate editor of *Contact* (with William Carlos
Williams). Both are correct: he was on *Contact*'s masthead
February, May and October 1932, and listed in *Americana* from
August through November 1933.

Note: Line 7, p. 4 (*The Dream Life of Balso Snell*) reads:
"O Anon! O Anan!"; it should read: "O Anon! O Onan!"

Additional American printings: Second printing, 22 May
1957 (with corrections in the introduction on p. x, but
others—such as the one on p. xxii that the publishers of
The Dream Life of Balso Snell went bankrupt—remain),
5,500 copies; third printing, 24 June 1957, 6,200 copies;
fourth printing, 13 June 1960, 3,000 copies; fifth printing,
16 December 1963, 2,300 copies; sixth printing, 1966.
Each printing, with the year, is so recorded on the verso
of the title-page.

Since the corrections in the second printing, the introduction and text have remained unchanged. With the third printing, the backstrip became brown cloth (instead of yellow). With the fifth printing, the entire cover became yellow (instead of black paper-covered boards), and the publisher's name was changed on the title-page to Farrar, Straus and Company, and on the spine to Farrar, Straus; the end-papers were white (instead of brown). With the sixth printing, the binding was changed to black cloth, and the publisher's name on the title-page to Farrar, Straus and Giroux, and on the spine in three lines (instead of one) to Farrar, / Straus & / Giroux /; the top edge was yellow (instead of black); the lettering on the spine was in gold (instead of white); and the price was raised to $6.00.

Reprintings:

a. *The Complete Works of* / NATH / ANAEL / WEST / Secker & Warburg: London / (Title covers two pages, with author's name on three uneven lines)

xxii, 421 [3] pp. 1957. 7 11/16 by 5 1/16 inches. Green cloth. Stamped in silver on spine: (rule) / Nathanael / West / (rule) / Complete / Works / Secker & / Warburg /. Printed from plates of the Farrar, Straus and Cudahy edition, second printing with differences on the title-page and verso, and changes made on p. x (of the introduction); and, of course, the binding. 25*s*. Reprinted 1968 at 45*s*.

First British Edition.

Translation:

b. *NATHANAËL WEST* / ROMANS / TRADUITS DE L'AMERICAIN / PAR MARCELLE SIBON / AVANT-PROPOS / DE MONIQUE NATHAN / *ÉDITIONS DU SEUIL* / *27, rue Jacob, Paris VI*ᵉ /

351 [1] pp. 1961. 8 1/16 by 5½ inches. Paperback.
Printed in green on front cover: NATHANAËL WEST
(in black) / Romans (in black) / Miss Lonelyhearts /
La vie rêvée de Balso Snell / L'incendie de Los Angelès /
Un million tout rond / traduits de l'américain / par
Marcelle Sibon / AUX ÉDITIONS DU SEUIL / (The
whole enclosed within green borders). Printed on spine:
Nathanael (in green) / *West* (in green) / *Romans*
(in black) / *Éditions du Seuil* (in green, reading
upwards) /. Printed in black (with title, author, and
publisher in green) on back cover: blurb for *Romans* in
33 lines and portrait of West. 28 fr.

Translation into French.

The order of the novels is not chronological, as in the American
edition, but rather odd: *Miss Lonelyhearts, Un million tout rond,
La vie rêvée de Balso Snell,* and *L'incendie de Los Angelès (The
Day of the Locust).*

  c. *Bulunmàz firsàtlar.* Translated by Faruk Sipahi. Istanbul:
Eskin Matbaasi, 1971. 156 pp. 800 kr.

Translation into Turkish. Not seen.

7. *Miss Lonelyhearts* (Play) (1959)

Miss / Lonelyhearts / BY HOWARD TEICHMANN /
ADAPTED FROM NATHANAEL WEST'S NOVEL /
* / A PLAY IN TWO ACTS / * / DRAMATISTS /
PLAY SERVICE / INC. / (The whole page has 7
vertical rules down the top left side, 7 horizontal lines
between the stars, and 7 vertical rules down the
bottom right side)

Collation: [1]-[80] pp., as follows: [1] title-page as above;
[2] notices: ©, COPYRIGHT, 1959, BY HOWARD
TEICHMANN / ©, COPYRIGHT, 1957, BY HOWARD
TEICHMANN / Based upon the novel, "Miss Lonely-

hearts," Copyright, 1933, / by Nathanael West /
(Copyright warning on 17 lines) / (Amateur acting
rights on 6 lines) /; [3] dedication: To the memory
of Nathanael West /; [4] blank; 5 foreword (signed:
Howard M. Teichmann); 6 cast of characters in the
original production, 3 October 1957; 7-76 text;
77-78 property plot; [79]-[80] advertisements for
Dramatists Play Service, Inc.

Issued in pink paper covers, stapled. Printed in black
on front cover: similar to material on title-page. Printed
in black on back cover: advertisement for Dramatists
Play Service, Inc. Printed in black on spine, reading
downwards: MISS LONELYHEARTS—Teichmann /.
Printed in black on inside of front and back covers:
advertisements for Dramatists Play Service, Inc. All edges
trimmed. The leaves measure 7¾ by 5¼ inches.

Published 1959. The original price was $1.00.
First edition.

B. Work by Nathanael West Originally Published in Books

1. *The Day of the Locust* (1950)

   NATHANAEL WEST / *The Day of the Locust* / WITH AN INTRODUCTION BY RICHARD B. GEHMAN / THE NEW CLASSICS /

   xxiv, 168 pp. New York: New Directions, 1950. 7 by 4¾ inches. Issued in light green cloth. Stamped in black on spine, reading downwards: THE DAY OF THE LOCUST /. New Classics No. 29. $1.50.

   Contains: Excerpts from "The Fake," later called "L'Affair Beano," pp. xiv-xv (in Richard B. Gehman's Introduction).

2. *F. Scott Fitzgerald and His Contemporaries* (1963)

   F. SCOTT / FITZGERALD *and* / *his contemporaries* / WILLIAM GOLDHURST / THE WORLD PUBLISHING COMPANY (publisher's device) / *Cleveland and New York* /

   252 pp. 1963. 8 by 5 inches. Issued in bright green cloth. Stamped in gold on front cover: F. SCOTT FITZGERALD / (rule in black) / *and his contemporaries* /. Stamped in gold on spine: GOLDHURST / (four rules in black) / F. SCOTT / FITZGERALD / *and his* / *contemporaries* / (six rules in black) / WORLD /. Legend on p. [4]: First edition. $4.50.

Contains: Letter from Nathanael West to F. Scott Fitzgerald, dated 5 April 1939, p. 236.

3. *Years of Protest* (1967)

YEARS OF / PROTEST / A Collection of American Writings of the 1930's / edited by Jack Salzman / BARRY WALLENSTEIN, ASSISTANT EDITOR / PEGASUS (publisher's device) NEW YORK / 448 pp. 1967. 8 by 5 inches. Issued in pale grayish green cloth. Stamped in blind, within a box: publisher's device. Stamped in gold on spine: YEARS / OF / PROTEST / (rule) / Salzman / and / Wallenstein / (publisher's device) / PEGASUS /. Reprinted in paperback, slightly revised, 1970.

Contains: "Miss Lonelyhearts and the Dead Pan" (early version from *Contact* 1 (May 1932): 13-21), pp. 406-412.

4. *Nathanael West: The Art of His Life* (1970)

Nathanael West / The Art of His Life / *by Jay Martin* / (publisher's device) / FARRAR, STRAUS AND GIROUX / NEW YORK /

[xxii], 436 pp. 1970. 8⅜ by 5½ inches. Issued in cream cloth. Stamped on spine reading downwards: *Nathanael West* / THE ART OF HIS LIFE (in red) / JAY MARTIN *Farrar, Straus and Giroux* (in black) /. $10.00.

Reprinted in paperback by Hayden Book Company, Inc., New York, 1971; and in England by Secker & Warburg, London, 1971.

Contains: Numerous statements, letters, excerpts from unpublished stories (see list below), film treatments and scripts (see list below), plays (see list below), and uncollected poems and prose (see list below), from

p. [xxi] (a letter to S. J. Perelman) to p. 406 (a quotation from West's treatment of the movie "Bird in Hand"), *passim*.

5. *Nathanael West: A Collection of Critical Essays* (1971)
NATHANAEL WEST / A COLLECTION OF CRITICAL ESSAYS / Edited by / *Jay Martin* / Prentice-Hall, Inc. (A Spectrum Book device) *Englewood Cliffs, N. J.* / [x], 280 pp. 1971. 8 by 5½ inches. Stamped in gold on spine, reading downwards: NATHANAEL WEST *Edited by* Jay Martin Prentice-Hall /. Stamped in gold on bottom of back cover, ISBN number: 0-13-950618-7. Twentieth Century Views Series. Reprinted in paperback, a Spectrum Book S-TC-94, $1.95, by Prentice-Hall, Inc., 1971.

Contains: "Through the Hole in the Mundane Millstone" (from the pamphlet), pp. 29-30; "Some Notes on Violence" (from *Contact* 1 (October 1932): 132-133), pp. 50-51; "Some Notes on Miss L." (from *Contempo* 3 (15 May 1933): 1, 2), pp. 66-67; and "Bird and Bottle" (from *Pacific Weekly* 5 (10 November 1936): 329-331), pp. 132-137.

6. *Nathanael West: The Cheaters and the Cheated* (1973)
Nathanael West: / The Cheaters and the Cheated / A Collection of Critical Essays / edited by David Madden / (publisher's device) / EVERETT / EDWARDS, inc. / POST OFFICE BOX 1060 / DELAND, FLORIDA 32720 /
[xxiv], 346 pp. 1973. 9 by 5⅞ inches. Issued in light green cloth. Stamped in silver on front cover: NATHANAEL WEST: / The CHEATERS / & (across two lines) the CHEATERS!! / David Madden /. Stamped in silver on spine, reading downwards:

NATHANAEL / WEST | (across two lines) The
CHEATERS / & (across two lines) the CHEATERS!! /
MADDEN / (publisher's device) (last two lines reading
across) /. $13.00.

Contains: "Christmass Poem" (from *Contempo* 3
(21 February 1933): 4), pp. 13-14.

C. Plays by Nathanael West (Unpublished)

1. *Good Hunting: A Satire in 3 Acts* (with Joseph Schrank). Produced by Jerome Mayer and Leonard S. Field at the Hudson Theatre, New York City on 21 November 1938; ran two performances. [Originally called *Gentlemen, the War!* later *Blow, Bugles, Blow*, and finally *Good Hunting*, it has never been published; but under its original title, subheaded *A Play in Three Acts*, it was copyrighted in 1937 and a copy is in the Library of Congress; see Jay Martin, *Nathanael West: The Art in His Life*, pp. 290-302; and Burns Mantle, *The Best Plays of 1938-39* (New York: Dodd, Mead and Company, 1939), pp. 427-428, for a brief synopsis and the cast of the play.]

2. *Even Stephen* (with S. J. Perelman). [Never produced. First called *Guardian Angel*, the MS is in the possession of S. J. Perelman, executor of Nathanael West's estate. See Jay Martin, *Nathanael West: The Art of His Life*, pp. 250-251.]

D. Movies by Nathanael West

For quotations from and a discussion of all these movies, see Jay Martin, *Nathanael West: The Art of His Life,* "Appendix / Nathanael West's Film Writing," pp. 401-406, and in the main narrative of the biography.

1. *Beauty Parlor.* Columbia Studios, 1933. [Never produced.]

2. *Return to the Soil.* Columbia Studios, 1933. [Never produced.]

3. *Advice to the Lovelorn.* Adapted from the novel, *Miss Lonelyhearts.* Screenplay by Leonard Praskins. 20th Century Pictures. Released 1933. [West did not work on the script, which bears little resemblance to the novel. In addition to Jay Martin's biography of West, pp. 208-209, see P. S. Harrison, *Harrison's Reports: A Motion Picture Service Devoted Chiefly to the Interests of Exhibitors* 15 (26 August 1933): 133, 136.]

4. *Ticket to Paradise* (with Jack Natteford). Republic Productions, 1936.

5. *Follow Your Heart* (with Lester Cole and Samuel Ornitz). Republic Productions, 1936.

6. *The President's Mystery* (with Lester Cole). Republic Productions, 1936.

7. [Race-horse story.] Republic Productions, 1936. [Never produced.]

8. *Gangs of New York*. Republic Productions, 1936-1937. [West did not get screen credit when it was released in 1938.]

9. *Jim Hanvey—Detective*. Republic Productions, 1936.

10. *Rhythm in the Clouds* (adaptation). Republic Productions, 1937.

11. *Ladies in Distress* (West's treatment rewritten by Darrell and Stuart McGowan). Republic Productions, 1937. [West did not get screen credit when it was released in 1938.]

12. *Bachelor Girl* (with others). Republic Productions, 1937. [Never produced.]

13. *Born to Be Wild*. Republic Productions, 1937. [The only script on which West worked entirely alone at Republic.]

14. *It Could Happen to You*. Republic Productions, 1937. [Republic Studio's version of *A Cool Million* with Sinclair Lewis's *It Can't Happen Here* and "immigrant sociology" (via Samuel Ornitz).]

15. *Orphans of the Street*. Republic Productions, 1937-1938. [West did not get screen credit when it was released.]

16. *Stormy Weather*. Republic Productions, 1937-1938. [Never produced.]

17. *Osceola*. [Original, probably written in 1935; never sold or produced.]

18. *Broadway Bible*. [Treatment for a musical screenplay, 1938; never sold or produced.]

19. *The Squealer*. Columbia Studios, 1938. [First-draft script never finished or produced.]

20. *Five Came Back* (with Jerry Cady and Dalton Trumbo). RKO Pictures, 1938, released 1939.

21. *Flight South*, later called *Heritage of the Wild* (with Gordon Kahn and Wells Root). MGM, 1938. [Treatment purchased but never produced.]

22. *The Spirit of Culver* (original by George Green, Tom Buckingham, and Clarence Marks; screenplay by Nathanael West and Whitney Bolton). Universal Corporation, 1939. [Typescript of the shooting script, New York Public Library, 164 pp.]

23. *I Stole a Million* (original by Lester Cole; screenplay by Nathanael West). Universal Corporation, 1939.

24. *The Victoria Docks at Eight* (original by Rufus King). Universal Corporation, 1939. [Never produced.]

25. *Before the Fact* (with Boris Ingster). RKO Pictures, 1939. [Rewritten by Alfred Hitchcock's staff and released as *Suspicion*.]

26. *Men Against the Sky*. RKO Pictures, 1940.

27. *Let's Make Music* (originally *Malvina Swings It*, by Charles Roberts). RKO Pictures, 1940.

28. *Stranger on the Third Floor* (final version by Nathanael West). RKO Pictures, 1940.

29. *A Cool Million: A Screen Story* (with Boris Ingster).
Columbia Studios, 1940. [Never produced.]

30. *Bird in Hand* (with Boris Ingster). RKO Pictures, 1940.
[Never produced.]

31. *Amateur Angel* (with Boris Ingster). Columbia Pictures,
1940. [Never produced.]

E. Work by Nathanael West Originally Published in Periodicals

All of the poetry and prose listed here is reprinted in Appendix, below.

1. "Rondeau." *The Brown Jug* (Brown University) Jugful No. 2 (December 1922): 24. [Poem unsigned. Reprinted in part in Jay Martin, *Nathanael West: The Art of His Life*, p. 74.]

2. "Euripides—A Playwright." *Casements* (Brown University) 1 (July 1923): [2-4]. [Essay, signed Nathanael v. W. Weinstein.]

3. "Death." *Casements* (Brown University) 2 (May 1924): 15. [Poem, signed N. von Wallenstein-Weinstein. Reprinted in Jay Martin, *Nathanael West: The Art of His Life*, p. 398.]

4. "A Barefaced Lie." *Overland Monthly and Out West Magazine* n.s. 87 (July 1929): 210, 219. [Short story. Signed N. West, this may or may not have been written by Nathanael West; for discussion, see notes listed below under W. Keith Kraus and William White in *American Notes & Queries*.]

46

5. "Book Marks for Today." *New York World Telegram,*
20 October 1931, p. 23. [Letter to the editor, with
Julian L. Shapiro. Reprinted in Jay Martin, *Nathanael
West: The Art of His Life,* p. 145.]

6. "Miss Lonelyhearts and the Lamb." *Contact* 1 (February
1932): 80-85. [Short story, basis for Chapter 3 of
Miss Lonelyhearts. Subtitled *An American Quarterly
Review* and published by Moss and Kamin, publishers of
The Dream Life of Balso Snell, the short-lived periodical
was edited by William Carlos Williams with
Nathanael West and Robert McAlmon as associate editors.]

7. "Two Chapters from Miss Lonelyhearts: Miss Lonelyhearts
and the Dead Pan [and] Miss Lonelyhearts and the
Clean Old Man." *Contact* 1 (May 1932): 13-21, 22-27.
[Short stories, bases for Chapter 2 and Chapter 5 of
Miss Lonelyhearts.]

8. "Miss Lonelyhearts in the Dismal Swamp." *Contempo*
(Chapel Hill, North Carolina) 2 (5 July 1932): 1, 2.
[Short story, basis for Chapter 8 of *Miss Lonelyhearts.*]

9. "Miss Lonelyhearts on a Field Trip." *Contact* 1 (October
1932): 50-57. [Signed Nathaniel West. Short story, basis
for Chapter 7 of *Miss Lonelyhearts.*]

10. "Some Notes on Violence." *Contact* 1 (October 1932):
132-133. [Essay, signed N. West. Reprinted in Jay Martin,
editor, *Nathanael West: A Collection of Critical Essays,*
pp. 50-51.]

11. "Christmass Poem." *Contempo* 3 (21 February 1933): 4.
[Poem. These 19 lines were part of a three-part 82-line
poem, "Burn the Cities," first published in Jay Martin,
Nathanael West: The Art of His Life, pp. 329-331.]

12. "Some Notes on Miss L." *Contempo* 3 (15 May 1933):
    1, 2. [Comments by West after the book's publication.
    Reprinted in Jay Martin, editor, *Nathanael West:
    A Collection of Critical Essays*, pp. 66-67.]

13. "Business Deal." *Americana* 1 (October 1933): 14-15.
    [Short story on Hollywood concerning a writer and a
    movie producer. *Americana*, published in New York by
    the Americana Group, was edited by Alexander King with
    Nathaniel [*sic*] West, George Grosz and Gilbert Seldes as
    Associates in its first issue, August 1933, containing an
    excerpt, "The Dear Public" (p. 29) from *The Dream Life
    of Balso Snell*; the September issue contained another one,
    "Excerpt" (p. 25), this time with West's name correct
    in both the masthead and the by-line. The next and final
    number of *Americana* 2 (November 1933) contained
    no articles signed by West.]

14. "Soft Soap for the Barber." *The New Republic* 81
    (14 November 1934): 23. [Book review of Gene Fowler,
    Father Goose: The Story of Mack Sennett.]

15. "Bird and Bottle." *Pacific Weekly* 5 (10 November 1936):
    329-331. [Short story, basis for Chapter 14 of *The Day
    of the Locust*. Reprinted in Jay Martin, editor, *Nathanael
    West: A Collection of Critical Essays*, pp. 132-137.]

16. Letter to F. Scott Fitzgerald. *Fitzgerald / Hemingway
    Annual* [3] (1971):302-303. [Dated 11 September 1934,
    the letter is a request for Fitzgerald's recommendation
    for West, who is applying for a Guggenheim Fellowship.]

F. Unpublished Stories and Other Writings by Nathanael West

1. "The Adventurer." [Excerpts in Jay Martin, *Nathanael West: The Art of His Life*, pp. 35-37, 50-51.]

2. "American Chauve Souris." [A "review or theatrical entertainment"; see outline, in part, in Jay Martin, *Nathanael West: The Art of His Life*, pp. 248-249.]

3. "Burn the Cities." [A three-part, 82-line poem, from which "A Christmass Poem" was taken; for the entire poem, see Jay Martin, *Nathanael West: The Art of His Life*, pp. 329-331.]

4. "The Fake," later "L'Affair Beano," and "The Imposter." [Excerpts in Richard B. Gehman, Introduction to *The Day of the Locust* (New York: New Directions, 1950), pp. xiv-xv; and Jay Martin, *Nathanael West: The Art of His Life*, pp. 88-90.]

5. "Mr. Potts of Pottstown." [Excerpts in Jay Martin, *Nathanael West: The Art of His Life*, pp. 168-170.]

6. "St. Pamphile: A Novelette."

7. "The Sun, the Lady, and the Gas Station." [Brief excerpts in Jay Martin, *Nathanael West: The Art of His Life*, pp. 171-172.]

8. "Three Eskimos." [Brief excerpts in Jay Martin, *Nathanael West: The Art of His Life*, p. 213.]

9. "Tibetan Night." [Brief excerpt in Jay Martin, *Nathanael West: The Art of His Life*, pp. 170-171.]

10. "Western Union Boy." [Excerpts in Jay Martin, *Nathanael West: The Art of His Life*, pp. 41-42, 55,268-269n.]

G. Selections from Nathanael West in Anthologies

1. *The American Writer and the Great Depression.* Edited by Harvey Swados. Indianapolis, New York, Kansas City: The Bobbs-Merrill Company, Inc. A Subsidiary of Howard K. Sams & Co., Inc., 1966, pp. 458-491.
   Contains: Chapters 13-23 (from *A Cool Million,* pp. 91-159).

2. *Years of Protest: A Collection of American Writings of the 1930's.* Edited by Jack Salzman; Barry Wallenstein, Assistant Editor. New York: Pegasus, Western Publishing Company, Inc., 1967, reprinted 1970, pp. 406-412.
   Contains: "Miss Lonelyhearts and the Dead Pan" (from *Contact* 1 (May 1932): 13-21).

3. *Contemporary American Thought: A College Reader.* Edited by E. W. Johnson. New York: The Free Press, 1968, p. 403.
   Contains: "Miss Lonelyhearts of Miss Lonelyhearts," (from *Miss Lonelyhearts,* pp. 128-129).

4. *The Literary Artist as Social Critic.* [Edited by] Thomas E. Kakonis and Barbara G. T. Desmarais. Beverly Hills, California: Glencoe Press, 1969, pp. 287-296.
   Contains: Chapter 27 (from *The Day of the Locust,* pp. 220-238).

5. *American Literature: Tradition & Innovation.* Edited by
   Harrison T. Meserole, Walter Sutton, and Brom Weber.
   Lexington, Massachusetts: D. C. Heath and Company, 1969,
   pp. 3276-3295.
   > Contains: "Miss Lonelyhearts, Help Me, Help Me",
   > "Miss Lonelyhearts on a Field Trip", "Miss Lonelyhearts
   > in the Dismal Swamp", "Miss Lonelyhearts and the
   > Cripple", "Miss Lonelyhearts Pays a Visit", and
   > "Miss Lonelyhearts Has a Religious Experience" (from
   > *Miss Lonelyhearts*, pp. 11-19, 97-112, 115-129, 161-172,
   > 175-184, and 209-215).

6. *Literature in America: The Modern Age.* Edited by Charles
   Kaplan. New York: The Free Press, 1971, pp. 285-296.
   > Contains: "Miss Lonelyhearts, Help Me, Help Me",
   > "Miss Lonelyhearts and the Dead Pan", "Miss Lonely-
   > hearts and the Lamb", and "Miss Lonelyhearts and
   > the Fat Thumb" (from *Miss Lonelyhearts*, pp. 11-55).

7. *Forms of Prose Fiction.* Edited by James L. Calderwood and
   Harold E. Toliver. Englewood Cliffs, N.J.: Prentice-Hall,
   Inc., 1972, pp. 259-267.
   > Contains: Chapter 27 (from *The Day of the Locust*,
   > pp. 220-238).

H. Biographical and Critical Material About Nathanael West

I. Books and Pamphlets

1. Comerchero, Victor. *Nathanael West: The Ironic Prophet.* Syracuse: Syracuse University Press, 1964. xii, 189 pp. [Reprinted as a Washington Paperback, Seattle and London: University of Washington Press, 1967.]

2. Cramer, Carter M. *The World of Nathanael West: A Critical Interpretation.* (The Emporia State Research Studies Vol. 19, No. 4.) Emporia: Kansas State Teachers College, 1971. 71 pp. [Pamphlet.]

3. Hyman, Stanley Edgar. *Nathanael West.* (University of Minnesota Pamphlets on American Writers No. 21.) Minneapolis: University of Minnesota Press, 1962. 48 pp. [Reprinted in William Van O'Connor, editor, *Seven Modern American Novelists: An Introduction* (Minneapolis: The University of Minnesota Press, 1964), pp. 226-263; also as a Mentor Book in paperback (New York and Toronto: The New American Library, 1968), pp. 211-244; and in part as an Introduction to *Miss Lonelyhearts* (New York: Avon Books, 1964), pp. 5-28; and as an Afterword to *Miss Lonelyhearts* (New York: Avon Books, 1965 and 1967), pp. 105-128.]

4. Jackson, Thomas H., editor. *Twentieth Century Interpretations of* Miss Lonelyhearts: *A Collection of Critical Essays.* Englewood Cliffs, N. J.: Prentice-Hall, Inc., 1971. ix, 112 pp. [Cloth and paperback editions.]
Contains:

Thomas H. Jackson, "Introduction," pp. 1-17.

James F. Light, "The Christ Dream," pp. 19-38, reprinted from *Nathanael West: An Interpretative Study*, pp. 74-98.

Josephine Herbst, "Nathanael West," pp. 39-45, reprinted from *The Kenyon Review* 23 (Autumn 1961): 611-630.

Arthur Cohen, "The Possibility of Belief: Nathanael West's Holy Fool," pp. 46-48, reprinted from *Commonweal* 64 (15 June 1956): 276-278.

Robert J. Andreach, "Nathanael West's *Miss Lonelyhearts*: Between the Dead Pan and the Unborn Christ," pp. 49-60, reprinted from *Modern Fiction Studies* 12 (Summer 1966): 251-260.

Robert I. Edenbaum, "To Kill God and Build a Church: Nathanael West's *Miss Lonelyhearts*," pp. 61-69, reprinted from *The CEA Critic* 29 (June 1967): 5-7, 11.

Stanley Edgar Hyman, "Nathanael West," pp. 70-80, reprinted from *Nathanael West*, pp. 16-29.

Edmond L. Volpe, "The Waste Land of Nathanael West," pp. 81-92, reprinted from *Renascence* 13 (Winter 1961): 69-77, 112.

Randall Reid, "No Redeemer, No Promised Land," pp. 93-96, reprinted from *The Fiction of Nathanael West: No Redeemer, No Promised Land*, pp. 82-83, 85-87.

Josephine Herbst, *"Miss Lonelyhearts*: An Allegory,"
pp. 97-98, reprinted from *Contempo* 3
(25 July 1933): 4.

Angel Flores, "Miss Lonelyhearts in the Haunted
Castle," pp. 98-99, reprinted from *Contempo* 3
(25 July 1933): 1.

William Carlos Williams, "Sordid? Good God!"
pp. 99-103, reprinted from *Contempo* 3
(25 July 1933): 5, 8.

5. Light, James F. *Nathanael West: An Interpretative Study.*
Evanston, Illinois: Northwestern University Press,
[1961]. xiii, 220 pp. [Second (revised) edition, 1971,
xxv, 236 pp.]

6. Madden, David, editor. *Nathanael West: The Cheaters and
the Cheated: A Collection of Critical Essays.* Deland,
Florida: Everett / Edwards, Inc., 1973. xxiii, 346 pp.
Contains:

David Madden, "Introduction: A Confluence of Voices,"
pp. xv-xxiii.

Gerald Locklin, "The Man Behind the Novels,"
pp. 1-15.

[David Madden] "A Confluence of Voices: *The Dream
Life of Balso Snell,*" pp. 17-22.

Gerald Locklin, *"The Dream Life of Balso Snell*:
Journey into the Microcosm," pp. 23-56.

John M. Brand, "A Word Is a Word Is a Word,"
pp. 57-75.

[David Madden] "A Confluence of Voices: *Miss
Lonelyhearts,*" pp. 77-82.

Lawrence W. DiStasi, "Aggression in *Miss Lonelyhearts*:
Nowhere to Throw the Stone," pp. 83-101.

7. Malin, Irving. *Nathanael West's Novels*. With a Preface
   by Harry T. Moore. (Crosscurrents / Modern Critiques.)
   Carbondale and Edwardsville: Southern Illinois University
   Press; London and Amsterdam: Feffer & Simons, Inc.,
   1972. xi, 141 pp.

8. Martin, Jay. *Nathanael West: The Art of His Life*. New
   York: Farrar, Straus and Giroux, 1970. xxi, 435 pp.
   [The authorized biography. English edition, London:
   Secker & Warburg, 1971. Reprinted as a paperback,
   New York: Hayden Book Company, Inc., 1971.]

9. Martin, Jay, editor. *Nathanael West: A Collection of
   Critical Essays*. (Twentieth Century Views.) Englewood
   Cliffs, N. J.: Prentice-Hall, Inc., 1971. ix, 176 pp.
   [Cloth and paperback editions.]
   Contains:

   Jay Martin, "Introduction," pp. 1-10.
   S. J. Perelman, "Nathanael West: A Portrait," pp. 11-12,
   reprinted from *Contempo* 3 (25 July 1933): 1, 4.
   Josephine Herbst, "Nathanael West," pp. 13-28,
   reprinted from *The Kenyon Review* 23 (Autumn
   1961): 611-630.
   Nathanael West, "Through the Hole in the Mundane
   Millstone," pp. 29-30, reprinted from an advertisement
   flyer for *The Dream Life of Balso Snell* (New York:
   Moss and Kamin, 1931).
   David D. Galloway, "A Picaresque Apprenticeship:
   Nathanael West's *The Dream Life of Balso Snell* and
   A Cool Million," pp. 31-47, reprinted from
   Wisconsin Studies in Contemporary Literature 5
   (Summer 1964): 110-126.

William Carlos Williams, "A New American Writer,"
pp. 48-49, reprinted from *Il Mare* 11 (21 January
1931): 4 (translated from the Italian of Edmundo
Dodsworth into English by John Erwin and
Jay Martin).

Nathanael West, "Some Notes on Violence," pp. 50-51,
reprinted from *Contact* 1 (October 1932): 132-133.

Carter A. Daniel, "West's Revisions of *Miss Lonelyhearts*," pp. 52-65, reprinted from *Studies in
Bibliography* 16 (1963): 232-243.

Nathanael West, "Some Notes on Miss L.," pp. 66-67,
reprinted from *Contempo* 3 (15 May 1933): 1, 2.

Angel Flores, "Miss Lonelyhearts in the Haunted Castle,"
pp. 68-69, reprinted from *Contempo* 3 (25 July
1933): 1.

Josephine Herbst, "*Miss Lonelyhearts*: An Allegory,"
pp. 69-70, reprinted from *Contempo* 3 (25 July
1933): 4.

William Carlos Williams, "Sordid? Good God!"
pp. 70-73, reprinted from *Contempo* 3
(25 July 1933): 5, 8.

Marcus Smith, "Religious Experience in *Miss Lonelyhearts*," pp. 74-90, reprinted from *Contemporary
Literature* 9 (Spring 1968): 172-188.

Edmond L. Volpe, "The Waste Land of Nathanael
West," pp. 91-101, reprinted from *Renascence* 13
(Winter 1961): 69-77, 112.

Marc L. Ratner, " 'Anywhere Out of This World':
Baudelaire and Nathanael West," pp. 102-109,
reprinted from *American Literature* 31 (January
1960): 456-463.

Philippe Soupault, "Introduction" to *Mademoiselle Côeur-Brisé* (*Miss Lonelyhearts*), pp. 110-113, reprinted from *Mademoiselle Côeur-Brisé* (*Miss Lonelyhearts*), pp. 7-13 (translated from French into English by Hannah Josephson).

Jay Martin, "The Black Hole of Calcoolidge," pp. 114-131, reprinted from *Nathanael West: The Art of His Life*, pp. 225-243.

Nathanael West, "Bird and Bottle," pp. 132-137, reprinted from *Pacific Weekly* 5 (10 November 1936): 329-331.

William Carlos Williams, "*The Day of the Locust*," pp. 138-139, reprinted from *Tomorrow* 10 (November 1950): 58-59.

Edmund Wilson, "The Boys in the Back Room," pp. 140-143, reprinted from *Classics and Commercials: A Literary Chronicle of the Forties*, pp. 51-56.

Carvel Collins, "Nathanael West's *The Day of the Locust* and Faulkner's *Sanctuary*," pp. 144-146, reprinted from *Faulkner Studies* 2 (Summer 1953): 23-24.

W. H. Auden, "West's Disease," pp. 147-153, reprinted from *The Dyer's Hand and Other Essays*, pp. 238-245.

Norman Podhoretz, "Nathanael West: A Particular Kind of Joking," pp. 154-160, reprinted from *Doings and Undoings: The Fifties and After in American Writing*, pp. 65-75.

Daniel Aaron, "Late Thoughts on Nathanael West," pp. 161-169, reprinted from *The Massachusetts Review* 6 (Winter-Spring 1965): 307-316.

10. Perry, Robert M. *Nathanael West's* Miss Lonelyhearts: *Introduction and Commentary.* (Religious Dimensions in Literature No. 10.) New York: The Seabury Press, 1969. 32 pp. [Pamphlet.]

11. Reid, Randall. *The Fiction of Nathanael West: No Redeemer, No Promised Land.* Chicago and London: The University of Chicago Press, 1967. ix, 174 pp. [Reprinted as a Phoenix Book in paperback, Chicago and London: The University of Chicago Press, 1971.]

12. Scott, Nathan A., Jr. *Nathanael West: A Critical Essay.* (Contemporary Writers in Christian Perspective.) Grand Rapids, Michigan: William B. Eerdmans, 1971. 47 pp. [Pamphlet.]

II. Chapters and Material in Books

1. Aaron, Daniel. *Writers on the Left: Episodes in American Literary Communism*. New York: Harcourt, Brace and World, Inc., 1961, pp. 175, 307, 432. [Refers to West's speech, "Makers of Mass Neuroses," given at a San Francisco writer's conference, 13 October 1936.]

2. Abrahams, Roger D. "Androgynes Bound: Nathanael West's *Miss Lonelyhearts*." In Thomas B. Whitbread, editor. *Seven Contemporary Authors: Essays on Cozzens, Miller, West, Golding, Heller, Albee and Powers*. Austin: University of Texas Press, 1966, pp. 49-72.

3. Allen, Walter. "The Thirties: America." *The Modern Novel in Britain and the United States*. New York: E. P. Dutton & Co., Inc., 1964, pp. 167-172.

4. ———. *The Urgent West: The American Dream and Modern Man*. New York: E. P. Dutton & Co., Inc., 1969, pp. 217-219. [Parallels in John Steinbeck's *Grapes of Wrath* and *The Day of the Locust*, "something like the ultimate ironical presentation of the American Dream."]

5. Ames, Stanley Edward, editor. *The 1924 Liber Brunensis*. Providence: Brown University, 1924, p. 142. [Nathaniel Von Wallenstein Weinstein, New York, N. Y. 'Pep'. "From his seat in U. H., 'Pep' looks across to the Dean's office and smiles placidly, for he is an easy going, genial fellow. Addicted to reading the latest and best, he introduced "Jurgen" and "De Maupassant" to us—for

which we are truly thankful. He passes his time in drawing exotic pictures, quoting strange and fanciful poetry, and endeavoring to uplift Casements. He seems a bit eccentric at times, a characteristic of all geniuses. To predict his future would indeed be a hard task, so we'll leave the answer to the crystal and the astrologer. May his slogan always be 'Honi soit qui mal y pense.' " No honors, activities, or organizations are cited.]

6. Angoff, Allan, editor. *American Writing Today: Its Independence and Vigor.* New York: New York University Press, 1957, pp. 168, 206. [From *The Times Literary Supplement*, London; West is listed among those "not much regarded in 1930", and he is placed in the "School of the Grotesque".]

7. Auden, W. H. "Interlude: West's Disease." *The Dyer's Hand and Other Essays.* New York: Random House, 1962, pp. 238-245. [Reprinted, with changes, from *The Griffin* 6 (May 1957): 4-11; reprinted in Jay Martin, editor, *Nathanael West: A Collection of Critical Essays*, pp. 147-153.]

8. Benét, William Rose, editor. "West, Nathanael." *The Reader's Encyclopedia.* New York: Thomas Y. Crowell Company, 1948, p. 1200. [Second edition, 1965, p. 1083.]

8a. Bergonzi, Bernard. *The Situation of the Novel.* London: Macmillan, 1970; Pittsburgh: University of Pittsburgh Press, 1971, pp. 83-84, 95, 98, 104.

8b. Bier, Jesse. *The Rise and Fall of American Humor.* New York [etc.]: Holt, Rinehart and Winston, 1968, pp. 230-233, 417-418. [See also pp. 210, 319, 347n, 356n, 421.]

9. Bleiber, Everett F., editor. *Checklist of Fantastic Literature.* Chicago: Shasta Publishers, 1948, p. 283. [Lists *A Cool Million* among "fantasy, weird, and science fiction books."]

10. Block, Maxine, editor. "West, Nathanael." *Current Biography: Who's News and Why, 1941.* New York: The H. W. Wilson Company, 1941, p. 912. [Eight lines, mainly on the death of West and his wife.]

11. Bracey, William. "West, Nathanael." In *The Encyclopedia Americana.* International Edition. New York: Americana Corporation, 1964, 28: 633-634.

12. Brown, John. "[Nathanael West]." *Panorama de la littérature contemporaine aux États-Unis.* Paris: Librairies Gallimard, 1954, pp. 141-142.

13. Burke, W. J., and Will D. Howe. *American Authors and Books, 1640 to the Present Day,* Augumented and Revised by Irving R. Weiss. New York: Crown Publishers, Inc., 1962, p. 792. [West's dates are given as 17 October 1902 and 21 December 1940; *Miss Lonelyhearts* is listed on p. 498. West is not mentioned at all in the 1943 edition, New York: Gramercy Publishing Co.]

14. Caldwell, Erskine. *Call It Experience: The Years of Learning How to Write.* New York: Duell, Sloan and Pearce, 1951, pp. 110-112. [On Caldwell's living at the Sutton Club Hotel in 1931 for three weeks, and a brief account of his relationship with West.]

15. Coates, Robert M. Introduction to *Miss Lonelyhearts.* New York: New Directions, 1946, pp. 1-7; 1950, pp. ix-xiv.

16. Connolly, Cyril. *The Modern Movement: One Hundred Key Books from England, France and America 1880-1950.* New York: Atheneum, 1966, pp. 73-74. [*Miss Lonelyhearts* is No. 76; with *The Great Gatsby* and *The Sun Also Rises* "the three finest novels of our century." See the exhibition catalog, Cyril Connolly's *One Hundred Modern Books* (Austin: The University of Texas, 1971), p. 89.]

17. Courtney, Winifred, editor. *The Reader's Adviser: A Guide to the Best in Literature*: 1. 11th Edition, Revised and Enlarged. New York and London: R. R. Bowker Company, 1968, pp. 490-491.

18. Cowley, Malcolm. *Exile's Return: A Narrative of Ideas.* New York: W. W. Norton & Company, 1934, pp. 230-233. [Refers to *Miss Lonelyhearts* as "a brilliant novel that had few readers."]

19. ———. *Exile's Return: A Literary Odyssey of the 1920's.* New York: The Viking Press, 1951, pp. 237-240. [A revision of the 1934 material; says that *The Day of the Locust* is "still the best of the Hollywood novels" and that *Miss Lonelyhearts* is "a tender and recklessly imaginative novel that had few readers," adding in a footnote: "When it was reissued after the author's death, *Miss Lonelyhearts* had a somewhat larger public."]

20. ———. "American Books Abroad." In Robert Spiller [and others], editors. *The Literary History of the United States.* New York: The Macmillan Company, 1948, 2:1378. [One sentence mentions West: "The French . . . were also discovering and publishing, in the midst of a paper shortage, American books that had been largely neglected at home; for example, the fantastic *Miss*

Lonelyhearts, by Nathanael West, which had been published here in 1933 and had promptly gone out of print."]

21. ———. Introduction to *Miss Lonelyhearts*. New York: Avon Books, 1959, pp. ii-iv, 96.

22. Fadiman, Clifton, editor, assisted by Charles Van Doren. *The American Treasury, 1455-1955*. New York: Harper & Brothers, 1955, p. 971. [Under "Teller of Tales," West is listed with a quotation from *Miss Lonelyhearts*: "He sat in the window thinking. Man has a tropism for order. Keys in one pocket, change in another. . . . All order is doomed, yet the battle is worth while."]

23. Fiedler, Leslie A. "The Breakthrough: The American Jewish Novelist and the Fictional Image of the Jew." In Joseph J. Waldmeir, editor, *Recent American Fiction: Some Critical Views*. Boston: Houghton Mifflin Company, 1963, pp. 84-109. [Reprinted from *Mainstream* 4 (Winter 1958): 15-35.]

24. ———. *Love and Death in the American Novel*. (A Meridian Book.) Cleveland and New York: The World Publishing Company, 1962 (Criterion Books, Inc., 1960), pp. 316-318, 461-467. [Says that Faye Greener in *The Day of the Locust*, who is modelled on Jean Harlow, is the most memorable and terrible woman in an American novel of the Thirties. For all of Fiedler's comments on West, see *The Collected Essays of Leslie Fiedler* (New York: Stein and Day, 1971), 2 volumes: *passim* (more than 50 references).]

25. ———. *Waiting for the End*. New York: Stein and Day, 1964, pp. 37, 45-46, 48, 49-51, 63, 64, 83, 108, 143, 226. [Writes that West's "long neglect by the official

critics of the period is now being overbalanced by his enthusiastic discoverers. . . . What has been restored to us is only another tragically incomplete figure, whose slow approach to maturity ended in death. . . . In West . . . humor is expressed almost entirely in terms of the grotesque, which is to say, on the borderline between jest and horror; for violence is to him technique as well as subject matter, tone as well as theme."]

26. ———. *The Return of the Vanishing American*. New York: Stein and Day, 1968, pp. 144, 147-149, 150, 158. [Comments on the Hollywood cowboy and Indian in *The Day of the Locust*.]

27. Fitzgerald, F. Scott. *The Great Gatsby*. With a New Introduction by F. Scott Fitzgerald. New York: The Modern Library, 1934, p. viii. [A mere mention, which pleased West: "But all that is less discouraging, in the past few years, than the growing cowardice of the reviewers. Underpaid and overworked, they seem not to care for books, and it is saddening recently to see young talents in fiction expire from sheer lack of a stage to act on: West, McHugh and many others." See West's letter to Fitzgerald in William Goldhurst, *F. Scott Fitzgerald and His Contemporaries*, p. 236.]

28. Gehman, Richard B. Introduction to *The Day of the Locust*. New York: New Directions, 1950, pp. ix-xiii. [Slightly revised from *The Atlantic Monthly* 186 (September 1950): 69-72); reprinted in the paperback edition of the novel (New York: Bantam Books, 1953), pp. x-xvi; reprinted again, 1957-1964, pp. ix-xx.]

29. Greenberg, Alvin. "Choice: Ironic Alternatives in the World of the Contemporary American Novel." In David

Madden, editor. *American Dreams, American Nightmares.*
Preface by Harry T. Moore. (Crosscurrents / Modern
Critiques.) Carbondale and Edwardsville: Southern Illinois
University Press, 1970, pp. 175-187.

30. Hart, James D. "West, Nathanael." *The Oxford Companion to American Literature.* Third Edition. London,
New York: Oxford University Press, 1956, p. 814.
[West was omitted from the first (1941) and second
(1948) editions; he is given 11 lines in the third, and
28 lines in the fourth (New York: Oxford University
Press, 1965), p. 906.]

31. Haydn, Hiram, and Edmund Fuller, editors. *Thesaurus
of Book Digests: Digests of the World's Permanent
Writings from the Ancient Classics to Current Literature.*
New York: Crown Publishers, 1949, p. 493. [A digest
of *Miss Lonelyhearts* and one paragraph on *The Day of
the Locust.*]

31a. Hays, Peter L. *The Limping Hero: Grotesques in
Literature.* New York: New York University Press, 1971,
pp. 84-86.

31b. Heiney, Donald, and Lenthiel H. Downs. "Nathanael
West (1903-1940)." *Recent American Literature After
1930.* (Essentials of Contemporary Literature of the
Western World, Vol. 4.) Woodbury, N.Y.: Barron's
Educational Services, Inc., 1974, pp. 240-244.

32. Hellman, Lillian. *An Unfinished Woman—a Memoir.*
Boston, Toronto: Little, Brown and Company, 1969,
pp. 63, 270. [A note on Dashiell Hammett in the hotel
run by West, a photo of West with others, and this
comment: "Pep West saw it (Hollywood) through his

own wonderfully original mind and wrote, in *The Day of the Locust*, the only good book about Hollywood ever written."]

33. Herzberg, Max J. [and others]. "West, Nathanael." *The Reader's Encyclopedia of American Literature.* New York: Thomas Y. Crowell Company, 1962, p. 1211.

34. Hoffman, Frederick J. *The Modern Novel in America, 1900-1950.* Chicago: Henry Regnery Company, 1951, pp. 115n, 129. [Two sentences on *The Day of the Locust*; Hoffman was preparing a book on West in the TUSAS (New York: Twayne Publishers) series at the time of his death in 1968.]

35. Hodgart, Matthew. *Satire.* (World University Library.) New York, Toronto: McGraw-Hill Book Company, 1969, pp. 226-227.

36. Johansen, Ib. "I. Nathanael West; II. *A Cool Million.*" In Jens Bøgh and Steffen Skovmand, editors. *Six American Novels: From New Deal to New Frontier.* Aarus: Akademisk Boghandel, 1972, pp. 43-81.

37. Kernan, Alvin K. "The Mob Tendency [in Satire]: *The Day of the Locust.*" *The Plot of Satire.* New Haven and London: Yale University Press, 1965, pp. 66-80. [Reprinted from *Satire Newsletter* 1 (Winter 1964): 11-20.]

37a. Klein, Marcus, editor. *The American Novel Since World War II.* Greenwich, Conn.: Fawcett Publications, Inc., 1969, pp. 190, 250, 252. [References to West in essays by Paul Goodman, John Hawkes, and William Phillips.]

38. Knoll, Robert, editor. *McAlmon and the Lost Generation: A Self-Portrait.* Lincoln: University of Nebraska Press,

1962, pp. 305, 361, 381-382. [*Balso Snell*, according to Robert McAlmon, "was, as Ezra Pound told me . . . the sort of thing we should get off our chests by the beginning of sophomore year in college. . . . Later, however, West redeemed himself by writing *Miss Lonelyhearts*, which was a brilliant production."]

39. ———. *Robert McAlmon: Expatriate Publisher and Writer.* (New Series No. 18.) Lincoln: University of Nebraska Studies, 1957, pp. 18, 84. [McAlmon, though associated with Contact Editions, had nothing whatever to do with *The Dream Life of Balso Snell.*]

40. Kronenberger, Louis, editor. "West, Nathanael." *Atlantic Brief Lives: A Biographical Companion to the Arts.* Boston, Toronto: Little, Brown and Company, 1971, p. 862.

41. Kunitz, Stanley J., and Howard Haycraft, editors. "West, Nathanael (1906?- Dec. 21, 1940)." *Twentieth Century Authors: A Biographical Dictionary of Modern Literature.* New York: The H. W. Wilson Company, 1942, p. 1500. [*First Supplement*, 1955, p. 1069, adds eight lines, mainly bibliographical.]

41a. Lewis, R. W. B. "Days of Wrath and Laughter." *Trials of the Word: Essays in American Literature and the Humanistic Tradition.* New Haven, London: Yale University Press, 1965, pp. 184-235. [See especially pp. 213-218.]

42. Light, James F. "West, Nathanael." In *Encyclopædia Britannica.* Chicago [etc.]: Encyclopædia Britannica, Inc., 1969, 23:418.

42a. Macdonald, Dwight. "No Art and No Box Office."
      Discriminations: Essays & Afterthoughts 1938-1974.
      New York: Grossman Publishers (The Viking Press),
      1974, pp. 252-261. [On the movie, *Lonelyhearts*. Reprinted
      from *Encounter* 13 (July 1959): 51-55.]

43.   Madden, David, editor. *Proletarian Writers of the Thirties.*
      Preface by Harry T. Moore. (Crosscurrents / Modern
      Critques.) Carbondale and Edwardsville: Southern Illinois
      University Press; London and Amsterdam: Feffer &
      Simons, Inc., 1968, pp. xvi, xxiv, xxv, 5, 8, 10, 13, 18, 19,
      142-145, 154. [See note below.]

44.   ———. *Tough Guy Writers of the Thirties.* Preface by
      Harry T. Moore. (Crosscurrents / Modern Critiques.)
      Carbondale and Edwardsville: Southern Illinois University
      Press; London and Amsterdam: Feffer & Simons, Inc.,
      1968, pp. 145, 161, 167, 199, 217. [In these two collections
      there is no essay on West, but he is mentioned several
      times by David Madden, Leslie Fiedler, and Marcus Klein;
      by Thomas Sturak, E. R. Hagemann, and Carolyn See.]

45.   Magny, Claude-Edmonde. *The Age of the American Novel:
      The Film Aesthetic of Fiction Between the Two Wars.*
      Translated by Eleanor Hochman. New York: Frederick
      Ungar Publishing Co., 1972, pp. 146, 225, 226, 229, 232.
      [From *L'age du roman américain* (Paris: Éditions du
      Seuil, 1948).]

46.   Mantle, Burns, editor. *The Best Plays of 1938-39 and the
      Year Book of Drama in America.* New York: Dodd,
      Mead and Company, 1939, pp. 427-428. [Gives a brief
      synopsis and the cast of the play, "Good Hunting:
      A Satire in 3 Acts" (by West and Joseph Schrank),
      produced by Jerome Mayer and Leonard Field at the

Hudson Theatre, New York, 21 November 1938;
ran two performances.]

46a. May, John R. "Words and Deeds: Apocalyptic Judgment
in Faulkner, West, and O'Connor." *Toward a New Earth:
Apocalypse in the American Novel*. Notre Dame, London:
University of Notre Dame Press, 1972, pp. 92-144. [See
especially pp. 114-126, and also 204-206, 209, 211, 213, 217,
220.]

47. McKenney, Ruth. *Love Story*. New York: Harcourt,
Brace and Company, 1950, pp. 175-176, 195-197. [On
her sister Eileen's marriage to West, their accident
and death.]

48. Millgate, Michael. *American Social Fiction: James to
Cozzens*. Edinburgh and London: Oliver & Boyd, 1964,
pp. 154-156, 163-164.

49. Murray, Edward. "Nathanael West—The Pictorial Eye
in Locust-Land." *The Cinematic Imagination: Writers
and the Motion Pictures*. New York: Frederick Ungar
Publishing Co., 1972, pp. 206-216.

50. Nathan, Monique. "Avant-Propos to Nathanael West,
Romans." Paris: Éditions du Seuil, 1957, pp. 7-12. [An
introduction to the French *Complete Works*.]

51. Nelson, Gerald B. "Lonelyhearts." *Ten Versions of America*.
New York: Alfred A. Knopf, 1972, pp. 77-90.

52. Nyren, Dorothy, compiler and editor. "West, Nathanael
(1906-1940)." *A Library of Literary Criticism: Modern
American Literature*. New York: Frederick Ungar
Publishing Co., 1960, pp. 514-517. Fourth Enlarged Edition,
compiled and edited by Dorothy Nyren Curley
[and others], 1969, 3:335-341.

53. O'Connor, William Van. *The Grotesque: An American Genre*. Preface by Harry T. Moore. (Crosscurrents / Modern Critiques.) Carbondale: Southern Illinois University Press, 1962, pp. 6, 8-9, 12, 18, 21, 55, 56.

54. Olsen, Bruce. "Nathanael West: The Use of Cynicism." In Charles Alva Hoyt, editor. *Minor American Novelists*. Preface by Harry T. Moore. (Crosscurrents / Modern Critiques.) Carbondale and Edwardsville: Southern Illinois University Press; London and Amsterdam: Feffer & Simons, Inc., 1970, pp. 81-94.

54a. Parkes, David L. "West, Nathanael." In Kenneth Richardson, editor. *Twentieth Century Writing: A Reader's Guide to Contemporary Literature*. London [etc.]: Newnes Books, 1969, p. 642.

55. Parry, Idris. "Kafka, Gogol, and Nathanael West." In Ronald Gray, editor. *Kafka: A Collection of Critical Essays*. Englewood Cliffs, N. J.: Prentice-Hall, Inc., 1962, pp. 85-90. [Reprinted from I. F. Parry, "Kafka and Gogol," *German Life and Letters* 6 (1953): 141-145.]

56. Podhoretz, Norman. "Nathanael West: A Particular Kind of Joking." *Doings and Undoings: The Fifties and After in American Writing*. New York: Farrar, Straus & Company, 1964, pp. 66-75. [Reprinted from *The New Yorker* 33 (18 May 1957): 144-153.]

57. Powell, Lawrence Clark. "Nathanael West: The Day of the Locust." *California Classics: The Creative Literature of the Golden State*. Los Angeles: The Ward Ritchie Press, 1971, pp. 344-356. [Reprinted from *Westways* 62 (November 1970): 12-15, 44.]

58. Pritchett, V. S. *"Miss Lonelyhearts." The Living Novel & Later Appreciations.* London: Chatto and Windus; New York: Random House, 1964, pp. 276-282. [Reprinted, revised, from *The New Statesman* 54 (7 December 1957): 791-792.]

58a. Raban, Jonathan. "A Surfeit of Commodities: The Novels of Nathanael West." In [Malcolm Bradbury and David Palmer, editors] *The American Novel and the Nineteen Twenties.* (Stratford-upon-Avon Studies 13.) London: Edward Arnold; New York: Crane, Russak, 1971, pp. 215-231.

59. Ramsey, Terry, editor. "West, Nathaniel [*sic*]." *1940-41 International Motion Picture Almanac.* New York: Quigley Publishing Co., 1940, p. 635. [Lists eight movies on which West worked, with dates and studios. In the 1941-42 issue, p. 1098, West's name appears under "Deaths of the Year."]

60. Ross, Alan. "An Introduction to Nathanael West." *Miss Lonelyhearts.* London: The Grey Walls Press, 1949, pp. 7-25. [Reprinted from *Horizon* 18 (October 1948): 284-296; reprinted, revised, in *The Complete Works,* both New York and London editions.]

61. ———. Einführung to *Schreiben Sie Miss Lonelyhearts.* Zürich: Diogenes Verlag, 1961, pp. 5-10; Frankfurt am Main and Hamburg: Fischer Bücherei, 1963, pp. 5-11. [Considerably reduced and translated into German from the Introduction to *The Complete Works.*]

62. ———. "West, Nathanael." In Geoffrey Grigson, editor. *The Concise Encyclopedia of Modern World Literature.* London: Hutchinson; New York: Hawthorn Books, Inc., 1963, p. 483; portrait, p. 473.

63. Schulberg, Budd. "The Writer and Hollywood." In John Fischer and Robert B. Silver, editors. *Writing in America.* New Brunswick, N. J.: Rutgers University Press, 1960, p. 97. [Reprinted from *Harper's Magazine* 219 (October 1959): 132-137; mentions West among those "hired hands I bumped into out there . . . (who had) a pictorial mind and a Rimbaud sense of savage imagery."]

64. ————. Introduction to *The Day of the Locust.* New York: Time Incorporated, 1965, pp. xiii-xxiii.

65. Schulz, Max F. "Nathanael West's Desperate Detachment." *Radical Sophistication: Studies in Contemporary Jewish-American Novelists.* Athens: Ohio University Press, 1969, pp. 36-55.

66. Scott, Nathan A., Jr. *Modern Literature and the Religious Frontier.* New York: Harper & Brothers, 1958, p. 74. [" 'The distance of God'—this might, indeed, be regarded as a major loss of many of the most memorable books of our time . . ., of Nathanael West's *Miss Lonelyhearts.*"]

67. Soupault, Philippe. Préface (Introduction) to *Mademoiselle Cœur-Brisé (Miss Lonelyhearts).* Paris: Éditions du Sagittaire, 1946, pp. 7-13. [Reprinted, translated from French, in Jay Martin, editor, *Nathanael West: A Collection of Critical Essays,* pp. 110-113.]

68. Spiller, Robert [and others], editors. *The Literary History of the United States.* New York: The Macmillan Company, 1948, 3:151. [West appears in one sentence in the bibliographical section: "Recent writers of fiction, together with a representative volume by each author, include . . . Nathanael West (1906-1940), *Miss Lonely-*

hearts (1933—reissued by New Directions, 1946) . . .". His
first name is misspelled in the index, and he is ignored
in the *Bibliographical Supplement*, 1962.]

69. Straumann, Heinrich. *American Literature in the Twentieth
Century*. London: Hutchinson's University Library, 1951,
pp. 80, 87. [A paragraph, mainly on *Miss Lonelyhearts*,
by a Swiss professor in a British publication at an
early date in West's recognition.]

69a. Swingewood, Alan. "Alienation, Reification, and the
Novel [Sartre, Camus, Nathanael West]." In Diana T.
Laurenson and Alan Swingewood, *The Sociology of
Literature*. New York: Schocken Books, 1972, pp. 207-248.

70. Symons, Julian. "The Case of Nathanael West." *Critical
Occasions*. London: Hamish Hamilton, Ltd., 1966,
pp. 99-105.

71. Tiusanen, Antero. Suomentanut to *Vastaathan kirjeeseeni,
Miss Lonelyhearts*. Porvoo, Helsinki: Werner Söderström
Osakeyhtiö, 1966, pp. [7-12]. [In Finnish.]

72. Walker, Franklin. *A Literary History of Southern
California*. (Chronicles of California Series.) Berkeley
and Los Angeles: University of California Press, 1950,
p. 259. ["A number of local writers . . . have turned
their attention to regional themes. . . . Of somewhat more
serious intent are the works of two promising writers
who died young—*The Day of the Locust*, by Nathaniel
(*sic*) West, and *The Last Tycoon* (by) F. Scott Fitzgerald.
Although they vary in degree of satire, humor, and
shock, the novels about Hollywood nearly all agree that
life in the movie colony is artificial, the art meretricious,
and the industry the graveyard of talent."]

72a. Weaver, Mike. *William Carlos Williams: The American Background*. Cambridge: At the University Press, 1971, pp. 134-136, 145, 216.

73. Weber, Brom. "The Mode of 'Black Humor.' " In Louis D. Rubin, Jr., editor. *The Comic Imagination in American Literature*. New Brunswick: Rutgers University Press, 1973, pp. 366-367. [Says of *The Dream Life of Balso Snell*: "Of all the young American avant-garde writers influenced by the dadaist-surrealist ferment in the 1920's, only one—Nathanael West—managed the feat of creating an extended work of black humor."]

74. Weber, J. Sherwood, editor. *Good Reading*. Prepared by the Committee on College Reading, National Council of Teachers of English. New York: R. R. Bowker Company, 1960, p. 132. [At the end of John William Ward, "20th Century American Novels," including 68 novelists, is a further list of "Additional Recommended Novels in Paperbound," a grudging inclusion of *The Day of the Locust* and *Miss Lonelyhearts*. A previous edition of the NCTE, *A Guide to Good Reading* (New York: Hendricks House—Farrar, Straus, 1948) does not list West at all.]

75. Wells, Walter. "Shriek of the Locusts." *Tycoons and Locusts: A Regional Look at Hollywood Fiction of the 1930s*. (Crosscurrents / Modern Critiques.) Preface by Harry T. Moore. Carbondale and Edwardsville: Southern Illinois University Press; London and Amsterdam: Feffer & Simons, Inc., 1973, pp. 49-70; see also pp. 11, 39, 71, 72, 73, 80, 84, 87, 94, 95, 100, 101, 103, 107, 109, 110, 117, 118, 119, 122, 125.

76. White, William. "Nathanael West." In Frank N. Magill, editor. *Cyclopedia of World Authors*, New York: Salem Press; New York: Harper & Row, 1958, pp. 1144-1145.

77. ———. "The Complete Works of Nathanael West," In Frank N. Magill [and] Dayton Kohler, editors, *Masterplots: 1958 Annual*, New York: Salem Press, 1958, pp. 55-59. [Reprinted in *Best Masterplots, 1954-1964*, 1964, pp. 103-106.]

78. ———. "Miss Lonelyhearts." In Frank N. Magill [and] Dayton Kohler, editors. *Masterplots: Five Hundred Plot-Stories and Essay Reviews, Third Series*. New York: Salem Press, 1960, pp. 664-667. [Reprinted in Combined Edition, 1960, 4: 1961-1964; and *Best American Fiction*, 1964, pp. 407-409.]

79. Widmer, Kingsley. "The Sweet Prophecies of Nathanael West." In Warren French, editor. *The Thirties: Fiction, Poetry, Drama*. DeLand, Florida: Everett Edwards, Inc., 1967, pp. 97-106.

80. Williams, William Carlos. *Autobiography*. New York: Random House, 1951, pp. 301-302. [Reminiscences, especially regarding *Contact*, and West's choice of a pseudonym.]

81. ———. *The Selected Letters*, edited with an Introduction by John C. Thirlwall. New York: McDowell, Oblensky, 1957, pp. 125, 126, 128.

82. Wilson, Edmund. "Postscript." *The Boys in the Back Room: Notes on California Novelists*. San Francisco: The Colt Press, 1951, pp. 67-72. [Reprinted, in part, from "Hollywood Dance of Death," *The New Republic* 89

(26 July 1939) : 339-340; reprinted as "Facing the Pacific," in *Classics and Commercials: A Literary Chronicle of the Forties* (New York: Farrar, Straus, 1950; London: W. H. Allen, 1951), pp. 51-56; in *A Literary Chronicle: 1920-1950* (Garden City, New York: Doubleday & Company, Inc., 1956), pp. 245-249; and in Jay Martin, editor, *Nathanael West: A Collection of Critical Essays*, pp. 140-143.]

83. Unsigned. *The Historical Catalogue of Brown University, 1764-1934*. Providence, Rhode Island: Published by the University, 1936, p. 813. [West is listed under Class of 1924 by the name of Nathan Wallenstein Weinstein, degree Ph. B., and: "Editor, *Americana* Magazine, writer. Author, *The Dream Life of Balso Snell*, 1931; *Miss Lonelyhearts*, 1933, etc. *Covici-Friede, 384 4th Ave., New York, N. Y.*"]

84. ———. *Historical Catalogue of Brown University: 1950 Edition*. Providence: Brown University, 1951, p. 216. [West is listed under Class of 1924, with an asterisk to indicate deceased: "*WEST Nathanael Ph.B. novelist and film writer Oct. 17, 1902-Dec. 22, 1940."]

III. Periodical Articles

1. Aaron, Daniel. "The Truly Monstrous: A Note on Nathanael West." *Partisan Review* 14 (February 1947): 98-106.

2. ———. "Late Thoughts on Nathanael West." *The Massachusetts Review* 6 (Winter-Spring 1965): 307-317. [Reprinted in Jay Martin, editor, *Nathanael West: A Collection of Critical Essays*, pp. 161-169.]

3. Alter, Robert. "The Apocalyptic Temper." *Commentary* 41 (June 1966): 61-66.

4. Andreach, Robert J. "Nathanael West's *Miss Lonelyhearts*: Between the Dead Pan and the Unborn Christ." *Modern Fiction Studies* 12 (Summer 1966): 251-260. [Reprinted in Thomas H. Jackson, editor, *Twentieth Century Interpretations of* Miss Lonelyhearts, pp. 49-60.]

5. Auden, W. H. "West's Disease." *The Griffin* 6 (May 1957): 4-11. [Reprinted in *The Dyer's Hand and Other Essays*; and in Jay Martin, editor, *Nathanael West: A Collection of Critical Essays*, pp. 147-153.]

6. Balke, Betty Tevis. "Some Judeo-Christian Themes Seen Through the Eyes of J. D. Salinger and Nathanael West." *Cresset* 31 (May 1968): 7, 14-18.

7. Bittner, William. "A la recherche d'un écrivain perdu." *Les Langues Modernes* 54 (July-August 1960): 274-282. [In English.]

80

8. Breit, Harvey. "Go West." *New York Times Book Review* 62 (24 March 1957): 8.

8a. Brown, Daniel R. "The War Within Nathanael West: Naturalism and Existentialism." *Modern Fiction Studies* 20 Summer 1974): 181-202.

9. Buckley, Tom. "The Day of the Locust: Hollywood, by West, by Hollywood." *New York Times Magazine*, 2 June 1974, pp. 10-12, 50, 52, 55, 56, 58, 68, 70, 72-73.

10. Buddingh', C. "Nathanael West." *Tirade* (Antwerp) 8 (1964): 506-514

10a. Burke, Tom. "And It Came to Pass, Just as Nathanael West Told Us: Hollywood Collapsed and Fell into This $88,000 Hole . . . The Day of the Day of the Locust," *Esquire* 82 (September 1974): 120-126, 174-175. [Subtitled "Futility and failed dreams, with a cast of hundreds, directed by John Schlesinger"; on the movie version being made of the novel.]

11. Bush, C. W. "This Stupendous Fabric: The Metaphysics of Order in Melville's *Pierre* and Nathanael West's *Miss Lonelyhearts*." *Journal of American Studies* 1 (October 1967): 269-274.

12. Carlisle, Henry. "The Comic Tradition." *The American Scholar* 28 (Winter 1958-59): 96-108.

13. Cohen, Arthur. "Nathanael West's Holy Fool." *The Commonweal* 64 (15 June 1956): 276-278. [Reprinted in Thomas H. Jackson, editor, *Twentieth Century Interpretations of* Miss Lonelyhearts, pp. 46-48.]

14. Collins, Carvel. "Nathanael West's *The Day of the Locust* and *Sanctuary*." *Faulkner Studies* 2 (Summer 1953): 23-24.

[Reprinted in Jay Martin, editor, *Nathanael West: A Collection of Critical Essays*, pp. 144-146.]

15. Daniel, Carter A. "West's Revisions of *Miss Lonelyhearts.*" *Studies in Bibliography: Papers of the Bibliographical Society of the University of Virginia* 16 (1963): 232-243. [Reprinted in Jay Martin, editor, *Nathanael West: A Collection of Critical Essays*, pp. 52-65.]

16. Donovan, Alan. "Nathanael West and the Surrealistic Muse." *Kentucky Review* 2 (February 1968): 82-95.

17. Edenbaum, Robert I. "To Kill God and Build a Church: Nathanael West's *Miss Lonelyhearts.*" *The CEA Critic* 29 (June 1967): 5-7, 11. [Reprinted in Thomas H. Jackson, editor, *Twentieth Century Interpretations of* Miss Lonelyhearts, pp. 61-69.]

18. ———. "A Surfeit of Shoddy: Nathanael West's *A Cool Million.*" *Southern Humanities Review* 2 (Fall 1968): 427-439.

19. Fiedler, Leslie A. [*A Cool Million* "a neglected book."] *The American Scholar* 25 (Autumn 1956): 478.

20. ———. "The Breakthrough: The American Jewish Novelist and the Fictional Image of the Jew." *Mainstream* 4 (Winter 1958): 15-35. [Reprinted in Joseph J. Waldmeir, editor, *Recent American Fiction: Some Critical Views*, pp. 84-109.]

21. ———. "Master of Dreams," *Partisan Review* 34 (Summer 1967): 339-356. [The influence of Freud and Kafka on Jewish-American writing can be seen in, among other places, *The Dream Life of Balso Snell*.]

22. Flavin, Robert J. "Animal Imagery in the Works of Nathanael West." *Thoth* 6 (Spring 1965) : 25-30.

22a. Frank, Mike. "The Passion of Miss Lonelyhearts According to Nathanael West." *Studies in Short Fiction* 10 (Winter 1973) : 67-73.

23. Galloway, David D. "Nathanael West's Dream Dump." *Critique: Studies in Modern Fiction* 6 (Winter 1963-1964) : 46-63.

24. ———. "A Picaresque Apprenticeship: Nathanael West's *The Dream Life of Balso Snell* and *A Cool Million*." *Wisconsin Studies in Contemporary Literature* 5 (Summer 1964) : 110-126. [Reprinted in Jay Martin, editor, *Nathanael West: A Collection of Critical Essays*, pp. 31-47.]

25. Geha, Richard, Jr. "*Miss Lonelyhearts*: A Dual Mission of Mercy." *Hartford Studies in Literature* 3 (1971) : 116-131.

26. Gehman, Richard B. "My Favorite Forgotten Book [*The Day of the Locust*]." *Tomorrow* 8 (March 1949) : 61-62.

27. ———. "Nathanael West: A Novelist Apart." *The Atlantic Monthly* 186 (September 1950) : 69-72. [Considerably reworked from *Tomorrow* 8 (March 1949) : 61-62. Revised and reprinted as an Introduction to *The Day of the Locust* (New York: New Directions, 1950), pp. ix-xxiii; and *The Day of the Locust* (New York: Bantam Books, 1953), pp. x-xvi.]

28. Gilmore, Thomas B., Jr. "The Dark Night of the Cave: A Rejoinder to [Alvin] Kernan on *The Day of the Locust*." *Satire Newsletter* 2 (Spring 1965) : 95-100. [See Alvin Kernan, below.]

28a. Graham, John. "Struggling Upward: *The Minister's Charge* [W. D. Howells] and *A Cool Million*." *Canadian Review of American Studies* 4 (Fall 1973): 184-196.

29. Hand, Nancy Walker. "A Novel in the Form of a Comic Strip: Nathanael West's *Miss Lonelyhearts*." *The Serif* 5 (June 1968): 14-21.

30. Hassan, Ihab H. "Love in the Modern American Novel: Expense of Spirit and Waste of Shame." *Western Humanities Review* 14 (Spring 1961): 149-161.

31. Hawkes, John. "Notes on the Wild Goose Chase" ("Symposium: Fiction Today"). *The Massachusetts Review* 3 (Summer 1962): 784-788. [Djuna Barnes, Flannery O'Connor and Nathanael West are "very nearly alone in their uses of wit, their comic treatments of violence, and their extreme detachment. . . . For Nathanael West, love is a quail's feather dragged to earth by a heart-shaped drop of blood on its tip, or the sight of a young girl's buttocks like an inverted valentine."]

32. Herbst, Josephine. "Hunter of the Doves." *Botteghe Oscure* 13 (1954): 310-344.

33. ———. "Nathanael West." *The Kenyon Review* 23 (Autumn 1961): 611-630. [Reprinted in Jay Martin, editor, *Nathanael West: A Collection of Critical Essays*, pp. 13-28, and Thomas H. Jackson, editor, *Twentieth Century Interpretations of* Miss Lonelyhearts, pp. 39-45.]

34. Hollis, C. Carroll. "Nathanael West and Surrealist Violence." *Fresco* 7 (Spring-Summer 1957): 5-13.

35. ———. "Nathanael West: Diagnostician of the Lonely Crowd." *Fresco* 8 (Fall 1957): 5-21.

84

84

36. ———. "Nathanael West and the Lonely Crowd."
    Thought 33 (Autumn 1958): 398-416.

37. Jacobs, Robert G. "Nathanael West: The Christology
    of Unbelief." *Iowa English Yearbook* 9 (Fall 1964): 68-74.

38. Kanters, Robert. "Nathanael West perdu et retrouve."
    Figaro Littéraire No. 799 (12 August 1961): 2.

39. Kernan, Alvin. "The Mob Tendency in Satire: *The Day
    of the Locust.*" *Satire Newsletter* 1 (Winter 1964): 11-20.
    [See editor's note, *Satire Newsletter* 1 (Spring 1964):
    71; and Thomas B. Gilmore, Jr., above. Reprinted in
    The Plot of Satire, pp. 68-80; see also his *The Cankered
    Muse: Satire in the English Renaissance* (New Haven:
    Yale University Press, 1959), pp. 1-36.]

40. Kraus, W. Keith. "Nathanael West: A Further
    Bibliographical Note." *The Serif* 4 (March 1967): 32.
    [A movie based on *Miss Lonelyhearts.*]

41. ———. "An Uncited Nathanael West Story." *American
    Notes & Queries* 5 (January 1967): 163-164. [See
    William White, *American Notes & Queries* 6 (January
    1968): 72-73; and 6 (April 1968): 128.]

42. ———. "Mr. Kraus to Mr. White on N. West."
    American Notes & Queries 6 (April 1968): 128.
    [See item above.]

43. Levart, Herman H. "Correspondence." *Western Review*
    20 (Spring 1956): 254-255. [Accuses Cyril Schneider
    of plagiarism, saying his article in the *Western Review* 20
    (Autumn 1955) 7-28, was taken without permission or
    acknowledgment from Mr. Levart's MA thesis. See
    Mr. Schneider's reply in the same issue and the
    Editor's note.]

44. Levin, Meyer. "The Candid Cameraman." *Esquire* 6
(December 1936): 133-142. [Reviews the movie, "The
President's Mystery," on which West collaborated,
stressing the political-social values. West's name is not
specified.—E. R. Hagemann.]

45. Liebling, A. J. "Shed a Tear for Mr. West." *New York
World Telegram*, 24 June 1933, p. 14. [On *Miss Lonely-
hearts* and Liveright's bankruptcy; see also the *New
York Evening Post*, 10 May 1933.]

46. Light, James F. "*Miss Lonelyhearts*: The Imagery of
Nightmare." *American Quarterly* 8 (Winter 1956):
316-327.

47. ———. "Author's Query [about West]." *New York Times
Book Review* 62 (11 August 1957): 21. [Also appearing
in the *New York Times* are notices of the play, "Miss
Lonelyhearts," starring Pat O'Brien, opening at the
Music Box Theatre on 3 October 1957, adapted by
Howard Teichmann from the novel.]

48. ———. "Violence, Dreams, and Dostoevsky: The Art of
Nathanael West." *College English* 19 (February
1958): 208-213.

49. ———. "Nathanael West, 'Balso Snell,' and the Mundane
Millstone." *Modern Fiction Studies* 4 (Winter
1958-1959): 319-328.

50. ———. "Genius on Campus: Nathanael West at Brown."
Contact No. 3 (1959): 97-111.

51. ———. "Nathanael West and the Ravaging Locust."
American Quarterly 12 (Spring 1960): 44-54.

86

52. Lokke, V. L. "A Side Glance at Medusa: Hollywood, the Literature Boys, and Nathanael West." *Southwest Review* 46 (Winter 1961): 35-45.

53. Lorch, Thomas M. "The Inverted Structure of *Balso Snell*." *Studies in Short Fiction* 4 (Fall 1966): 33-41.

54. ———. "West's *Miss Lonelyhearts*: Skepticism Mitigated?" *Renascence* 18 (Winter 1966): 99-109.

55. ———. "Religion and Art in *Miss Lonelyhearts*." *Renascence* 20 (Autumn 1967): 11-17.

56. Lund, Mary Graham. "Backward-Forward in Forbidden Lands." *Western World Review* 3 (Spring 1968): 21-27.

56a. Macdonald, Dwight. "No Art and No Box Office." *Encounter* 13 (July 1959): 51-55. [On the movie, *Lonelyhearts*. Reprinted in *Discriminations*, pp. 252-261.]

57. Martin, Jay. "Fitzgerald Recommends Nathanael West for a Guggenheim." *Fitzgerald/Hemingway Annual* [3] (1971): 302-304. [Includes West's letter to Fitzgerald, 11 September 1934.]

58. McLaughlin, Richard. "West of Hollywood." *Theatre Arts* 35 (August 1951): 46-47. [Mainly on *The Day of the Locust*, much of the material from Gehman.]

59. Mjøberg, Jøran. "Nathanael West: En ironisk papetiker." *Bonniers Litterara Magasin* (Stockholm) 25 (1956): 133-137.

60. Nichols, James W. "Nathanael West, Sinclair Lewis, Alexander Pope and Satiric Contrasts." *Satire Newsletter* 5 (Spring 1968): 119-122.

60a. Orvell, Miles D. "The Messianic Sexuality of 'Miss Lonelyhearts.' " *Studies in Short Fiction* 10 (Spring 1973): 159-167.

61. Parry, Idris. "Kafka and Gogol." *German Life and Letters* 6 (1953): 141-145 [Reprinted in Ronald Gray, editor, *Kafka: A Collection of Critical Essays*, pp. 85-90.]

62. Perelman, S. J. "Nathanael West: A Portrait." *Contempo* 3 (25 July 1933): 1, 4. [Reprinted in *The Massachusetts Review* 6 (Winter-Spring 1965): 317; and in Jay Martin, editor, *Nathanael West: A Collection of Critical Essays*, pp. 11-12.]

63. Petrullo, Helen B. "Clichés and Three Political Satires of the Thirties." *Satire Newsletter* 8 (Spring 1971): 109-117.

64. Phillips, Robert S. "Fitzgerald and *The Day of the Locust.*" *Fitzgerald Newsletter* No. 15 (Fall 1961): 2-3.

65. Pinsker, Sanford, "Charles Dickens and Nathanael West: Great Expectations Unfulfilled." *Topic* 18 (1969): 40-52.

66. Pisk, George M. "The Graveyard of Dreams: A Study of Nathanael West's Last Novel, *The Day of the Locust.*" *South Central Bulletin* 27 (Winter 1967): 64-72.

67. Popkin, Henry. "Nathanael West." *Times Literary Supplement*, 11 April 1958, p. 195. [See below, Unsigned, "Nathanael West," *Times Literary Supplement.*]

68. Powell, Lawrence Clark. "California Classics Reread: Nathanael West's *The Day of the Locust.*" *Westways* 62 (November 1970): 12-15, 44. [Reprinted in *California Classics*, pp. 344-356.]

69. Ratner, Marc L. " 'Anywhere Out of This World': Baudelaire and Nathanael West." *American Literature* 31

(January 1960) : 456-463. [Reprinted in Jay Martin, editor, *Nathanael West: A Collection of Critical Essays*, pp. 102-109.]

70. Reynolds, Quentin. "When 'Pep' Was a Ghost." *Brown Alumni Monthly* 58 (December 1957) : 8-9. [Subtitled: "Nathanael West's Part in a Famous Spring Day Is Revealed as His Books Enjoy a Second Vogue."]

71. Richardson, Robert D., Jr. "Miss Lonelyhearts." *University of Kansas City Review* 33 (Winter 1966) : 151-157.

72. Rosenfeld, Isaac. "Faulkner and Contemporaries." *Partisan Review* 18 (January-February 1951) : 106-114.

73. Ross, Alan. "The Dead Centre: An Introduction to Nathanael West." *Horizon* 18 (October 1948) : 284-296. [Reprinted as an Introduction to *Miss Lonelyhearts* (London: The Grey Walls Press, 1949), pp. 7-25; and, revised, to *The Complete Works*, pp. vii-xxii.]

74. Sanford, John. [Julian L. Shapiro]. "Nathanael West." *The Screen Writer* 2 (December 1946) : 10-13. [A memorial essay by a personal friend on the sixth anniversary of West's death.]

75. Sasahara, Akira. "The World of *Miss Lonelyhearts*." *Essays and Studies in English Language and Literature* (Tohoku Gakuin University, Sendai, Japan) 53-54 (1968) : 109-130. [In Japanese.]

76. Schneider, Cyril M. "The Individuality of Nathanael West." *Western Review* 20 (Autumn 1955) : 7-28. [See Herman H. Levart, "Correspondence." *Western Review* 20 (Spring 1956) : 254-255; and following notes by Mr. Schneider and the Editor.]

77. Schulberg, Budd. "The Writer and Hollywood." *Harper's Magazine* 219 (October 1959): 132-137. [Reprinted in *Writing in America*, p. 97.]

78. Schrank, Joseph. "Pep." *New York Times Book Review* 62 (9 June 1957): 30. [On West's nickname.]

79. Schwartz, Edward Greenfield. "The Novels of Nathanael West." *Accent* 17 (Autumn 1957): 251-262.

80. Shepard, Douglas H. "Nathanael West Rewrites Horatio Alger, Jr." *Satire Newsletter* 3 (Fall 1965): 13-28.

81. Skerret, Joseph Taylor, Jr. "Dostoievsky, Nathanael West, and Some Contemporary American Fiction." *University of Dayton Review* 4 (Winter 1967): 23-25.

82. Smith, Marcus. "Religious Experience in *Miss Lonelyhearts*." *Contemporary Literature* 9 (Spring 1968): 172-188. [Reprinted in Jay Martin, editor, *Nathanael West: A Collection of Critical Essays*, pp. 74-90.]

83. Solberg, S. E. "The Novels of Nathaniel [*sic*] West: A Sargasso of the Imagination." *The English Language and Literature* (Seoul, Korea) No. 14 (1963): 125-146.

84. Steiner, T. R. "West's Lemuel and the American Dream." *The Southern Review* n.s. 7 (October 1971): 994-1006. [Reprinted in David Madden, editor, *Nathanael West: The Cheaters and the Cheated*, pp. 157-170.]

85. Tibbets, A. M. "The Strange Half-World of Nathanael West." *Prairie Schooner* 34 (Spring 1960): 8-14.

86. ———. "Nathanael West's *The Dream Life of Balso Snell*." *Studies in Short Fiction* 2 (Winter 1965): 105-112.

87. Van Voorhees, Archibald. "The Happy Mortician." *Saturday Review* 40 (11 May 1957): 13.

88. Volpe, Edmond L. "The Waste Land of Nathanael West." *Renascence* 13 (Winter 1961): 69-77, 112. [Reprinted in Thomas H. Jackson, editor, *Twentieth Century Interpretations of* Miss Lonelyhearts, pp. 81-92.]

89. White, William. "How Forgotten Was Nathanael West?" *American Book Collector* 8 (December 1957): 13-17.

90. ———. "Nathanael West: A Bibliography." *Studies in Bibliography: Papers of the Bibliographical Society of the University of Virginia* 11 (1958): 207-224.

91. ———. "A Novelist Ahead of His Time: Nathanael West." *Today's Japan: Orient/West* (Tokyo) 6 (January 1961): 55-64.

92. ———. "Some Uncollected Authors, XXXII: Nathanael West, 1903?-1940." *The Book Collector* 11 (Summer 1962): 206-210. [See also *The Book Collector* 11 (Autumn 1962): 315.]

93. ———. "Nathanael West: A Bibliography: Addenda (1957-1964)." *The Serif* 2 (March 1965): 5-18. [See *The Serif* 2 (September 1965): 28-31.]

94. ———. "Unpublished Faulkner: Reply to a Nathanael West Questionnaire." *American Book Collector* 17 (September 1966): 27.

95. ———. Review of *Studies in Bibliography* 11 (1958). *Bulletin of Bibliography* 23 (January-April 1958): 104. [Lists misprints in the West bibliography.]

96. ———. "Nathanael West." *Times Literary Supplement*, 21 February 1958, p. 101. [See below, Unsigned, *Times Literary Supplement*.]

97. ———. "Nathanael West." *Times Literary Supplement*, 9 May 1958, p. 255. [See below, Unsigned, *Times Literary Supplement*.]

98. ———. "The Plastered Duchess [and Nathanael West]." *Brown Alumni Monthly* 60 (April 1960): 22. [See "The Plastered Duchess," *Brown Alumni Monthly* 60 (March 1960): 26, which lists West as "Macaroni" in the Brown University play, 17 March 1924.]

99. ———. "Bibliography of Nathanael West." *The Book Collector* 11 (Autumn 1962): 351. [See *The Book Collector* 11 (Summer 1962): 206-210.]

100. ———. "Ernest Hemingway & Nathanael West: How Well Known Is Your Collector's Item?" *American Book Collector* 14 (May 1964): 29.

101. ———. "Nathanael West: Further Bibliographical Notes." *The Serif* 2 (September 1965): 28-31. [See *The Serif* 2 (March 1965): 5-18.]

102. ———. "Nathanael West's 'Balso Snell' in Cloth." *The Papers of the Bibliographical Society of America* 60 (October-December 1966): 474-476.

103. ———. "Notes on Hemingway, West, Tolkien, Wise." *American Book Collector* 18 (January-February 1968): 30-31.

104. ———. " 'Uncited West Story': A Dissent." *American Notes & Queries* 6 (January 1968): 72-73. [See W. Keith Kraus items above.]

105. ———. " 'Go West!' Notes from a Bibliographer."
American Book Collector 19 (January 1969): 7-10.

106. ———. "Nathanael West's *A Cool Million*." *American
Notes & Queries* 8 (April 1970): 120.

107. ———. "Fate and Nathanael West: A 1970 Note."
Literary Sketches 10 (October 1970): 6-7.

108. ———. "Nathanael West: A Working Checklist."
Bulletin of Bibliography 29 (October-December
1972): 140-143.

109. ———. "*Miss Lonelyhearts*: You've Read the Book,
Now See the Movie." *American Book Collector* 24
(November-December 1973): 31-32.

110. Widmer, Kingsley. "The Hollywood Image."
Coastlines 5 (Autumn 1961): 17-27.

111. Williams, William Carlos. "A New American Writer"
("Un nuovo scrittore americano"). *Il Mare* 11 (21 January
1931): 4. [Translated into Italian by Edmundo
Dodsworth. Reprinted (in English, by John Erwin and
Jay Martin) in Jay Martin, editor, *Nathanael West:
A Collection of Critical Essays*, pp. 48-49.]

112. ———. "The Contact Story." *Contact* No. 1 (1959):
75-77.

113. Wilson, Edmund. "Hollywood Dance of Death."
The New Republic 89 (26 July 1939): 339-340.
[Reprinted in part in *The Boys in the Back Room*.]

114. Your Reviewer. "Nathanael West." *Times Literary
Supplement*, 28 February 1958, p. 115. [See below,
Unsigned, *Times Literary Supplement*.]

114a. Zimmer, Dieter. "Nathanael West oder Warnungen vorm Tag der Heuschrecken." *Newe Rundschau* 83 (No. 2, 1972): 287-302.

115. Zlotnick, Joan. "The Medium Is the Message, Or Is It? A Study of Nathanael West's Comic Strip Novel." *Journal of Popular Culture* 5 (Summer 1971): 236-240.

116. Unsigned, "Nathanael West." *Times Literary Supplement,* 24 January 1958, p. 44. [Review of *The Complete Works.* Followed by a series of letters: William White, 21 February 1958, p. 101: Your Reviewer, 28 February 1958, p. 115; Henry Popkin, 11 April 1958, p. 195; and William White, 9 May 1958, p. 255.]

117. ———. *The New York Times,* 23 December 1940, p. 23. [' "My Sister Eileen" / Killed in Accident / Subject of Ruth McKenney Play / and Husband Die in West / El Centro, Calif., Dec. 22 (AP)—Nathaniel West, 34 years old, novelist and screen writer, and his wife, Eileen, of North Hollywood. . . .']

118. ———. *The Publishers' Weekly* 138 (28 December 1940): 2326. [Under "Obituary Notes: Nathanael West," gives 17 lines, listing his four books and screen play adaptation "Advice to the Lovelorn," and errs in his death date as 21 December and his age as 34.]

119. ———. *Los Angeles Times,* 23 December 1940, Part 2, p. 1. ["Scenario Writer and Wife Killed in Auto Collision (7-column banner) / Nathaniel W. Wests / Both Known for Work / in Hollywood Studios." Among errors are his name as Nathaniel W. West, his age as 36, and the title of one of his novels as "Miss Lonely Hearts." In the *Los Angeles Times,* 26 December

1940, Part 1, p. 9, under "Deaths" is: "West, Nathaniel W. / Pierce Brothers' Hollywood. 5959 / Santa Monica Blvd." No other data given.]

120. ———. *Imperial Valley Press* (El Centro, California), 23 December 1940, p. 1. [Photograph with heading: "Where Two Died, Three Met Injuries Sunday."]

IV. Reviews of Individual Books

The Dream Life of Balso Snell (1933)

1. G[aroffolo], N. G. [*The Dream Life of Balso Snell*].
   Contempo 1 (21 August 1931): 3.

Miss Lonelyhearts (1933)

2. Britten, Florence Haxton. "Grotesquely Beautiful Novel."
   New York Herald Tribune Books 9 (30 April 1933): 6.

3. Brown, Bob. "Go West, Young Writer!" *Contempo* 3
   (25 July 1933): 4-5. [This was one of several reviews
   in this issue under the general heading "*Miss Lonelyhearts*
   Is Reviewed." Also a sketch by S. J. Perelman and ads
   for the book.]

4. Caldwell, Erskine. [Comments on *Miss Lonelyhearts*
   in an ad.] *Contempo* 3 (15 May 1933): 7. [This same ad
   appeared in the 25 July 1933 issue, but this time
   Harcourt, Brace had been substituted for Liveright as
   the publisher. Four other writers are quoted. *Contempo* 3
   (15 March 1933): 2, mentions *Miss Lonelyhearts*
   having been accepted for publication by Liveright.]

5. Coates, Robert M. [Comments on *Miss Lonelyhearts* in an ad.] *Contempo* 3 (15 May 1933): 7.

6. ———. "Messiah of the Lonelyhearts." *The New Yorker* 9 (15 April 1933): 59.

7. D[avies], H[ugh] S[ykes]. "American Periodicals." *The Criterion* 11 (July 1932): 772-[775]. [Reviews the issue of *Contact*, February 1932, containing West's story "of the clumsy sacrificial slaughter of a lamb by drunken students."]

8. Flores, Angel. "Miss Lonelyhearts in the Haunted Castle." *Contempo* 3 (25 July 1933): 1. [Reprinted in Thomas H. Jackson, editor, *Twentieth Century Interpretations of* Miss Lonelyhearts, pp. 98-99; and in Jay Martin, editor, *Nathanael West: A Collection of Critical Essays,* pp. 68-69].

9. Hammett, Dashiell. [Comments on *Miss Lonelyhearts* in an ad.] *Contempo* 3 (15 May 1933): 7.

10. Herbst, Josephine. [Comments on *Miss Lonelyhearts* in an ad.] *Contempo* 3 (15 May 1933): 7.

11. ———. "Miss Lonelyhearts: An Allegory." *Contempo* 3 (25 July 1933): 4. [Reprinted in Thomas H. Jackson, editor, *Twentieth Century Interpretations of* Miss Lonelyhearts, pp. 97-98; and in Jay Martin, editor, *Nathanael West: A Collection of Critical Essays,* pp. 69-70.]

12. Matthews, T. S. "Novels—A Fortnight's Grist." *The New Republic* 74 (26 April 1933): 314-315.

13. Mott, Frank Luther. [*Miss Lonelyhearts.*] *Journalism Quarterly* 10 (June 1933): 120.

14. Troy, William. "Four Newer Novelists," *The Nation*, 136 (14 June 1933): 672-673.

15. Williams, William Carlos. "Sordid? Good God!" *Contempo* 3 (25 July 1933): 5, 8. [Reprinted in Thomas H. Jackson, editor, *Twentieth Century Interpretations of* Miss Lonelyhearts, pp. 98-99; and in Jay Martin, editor, *Nathanael West: A Collection of Critical Essays*, pp. 70-73].

16. Wilson, T. C. "American Humor," *Saturday Review of Literature* 9 (13 May 1933): 589.

17. Unsigned. [*Miss Lonelyhearts.*] *Boston Transcript*, 26 July 1933, p. 2.

18. ———. "Books and Reviews." *New Outlook* 162 (July 1933): 55, 58.

19. ———. " 'Miss Lonelyhearts' and Some Other Recent Works of Fiction." *New York Times Book Review* 37 (23 April 1933): 6.

A Cool Million (1934)

20. Britten, Florence Haxton. "Youth Against Age in Recent Leading Fiction," *New York Herald Tribune Books*, 10 (1 July 1934), 8-9.

21. Brickell, Herschel. [*A Cool Million*]. *New York Post*, 23 June 1934, p. 7.

22. Chamberlain, John. "Books of the Times," *The New York Times*, 19 June 1934, p. 17.

23. Gannett, Lewis. [*A Cool Million*]. *New York Herald Tribune*, 21 June 1934, p. 19.

24. Marsh, Fred T. "A Cool Million and Other Recent Works of Fiction." *New York Times Book Review* [29] (1 July 1934): 6.

25. Matthews, T. S. "A Gallery of Novels." *The New Republic* 79 (18 July 1934): 271.

26. S[tevens], G[eorge]. "The New Books." *Saturday Review of Literature* 10 (30 June 1934): 784.

27. Unsigned. [*A Cool Million*]. *Boston Transcript*, 14 July 1934, p. 2.

28. ———. "Shorter Notices." *The Nation* 139 (25 July 1934): 112.

29. ———. "In the Jungle." *Review of Reviews* 90 (August 1934): 6-7.

30. ———. "Brief Review." *New Masses* 12 (21 August 1934): 25.

The Day of the Locust (1939)

31. Britten, Florence Haxton. "New Novels from Far and Near." *New York Herald Tribune Books* 15 (21 May 1939): 7.

32. Fadiman, Clifton. "Books: Assorted Fiction." *The New Yorker* 15 (20 May 1939): 78-80.

33. Milburn, George. "The Hollywood Nobody Knows."
Saturday Review of Literature 20 (20 May 1939): 14-15.

34. Salomon, Louis B. "California Grotesque." *The Nation*
149 (15 July 1939): 78-79.

34a. Schulberg, Budd. "The Hollywood Novel." *Films* 1
(Spring 1940): 68-78. [On eight Hollywood novels,
including West's.]

35. Van Gelder, Robert. "A Tragic Chorus." *New York
Times Book Review* 44 (21 May 1939): 6-7.

36. Wilson, Edmund. "Hollywood Dance of Death." *The
New Republic* 99 (26 July 1939): 339-340. (Reprinted
in part in *The Boys in the Back Room*.)

37. Unsigned. "Truly Monstrous." *Time* 33 (19 June 1939): 84.

Miss Lonelyhearts (London, 1949)

38. Swann, Michael. "New Novels." *The New Statesman
and Nation* (London) 38 (6 August 1949): 153-154.

The Day of the Locust (1950)

39. Aaron, Daniel. "Writing for Apocalypse." *Hudson
Review* 3 (Winter 1951): 634-636.

40. Friedman, Robert. [*The Day of the Locust*]. *Daily Worker*, 23 November 1950.

41. Guilfoil, Kelsey. *Chicago Sunday Tribune*.

42. Markfield, Wallace. "From the Underbelly." *The New Leader* 33 (27 November 1950): 25.

43. Rosenfeld, Isaac. "Faulkner and Contemporaries." *Partisan Review* 18 (January-February 1951): 106-114.

44. Schulberg, Budd. "Feeble Bodies, Disordered Minds." *New York Times Book Review* 55 (10 October 1950): 4 [portrait].

46. Williams, William Carlos. [*The Day of the Locust*]. *Tomorrow* 10 (November 1950): 58-59.

47. Unsigned. "Neglected Novelist." *Newsweek* 36 (4 September 1950): 77-78.

The Complete Works (1957)

48. Bellamy, W. J. *Cambridge Quarterly* 4 (No. 1, 1968): 95-106.

49. Berolzheimer, H. F. *Library Journal* 82 (1 June 1957): 1539.

50. Bittner, William. "Catching Up With Nathanael West." *The Nation* 184 (4 May 1957): 394-396.

51. Coates, Robert M. "The Four Novels of Nathanael West, That Fierce, Humane Moralist." *New York Herald Tribune Book Review* 33 (9 May 1957): 4.

52. Cowley, Malcolm. "It's the Telling That Counts." *New York Times Book Review* 62 (12 May 1957): 4-5. [Portrait.]

53. Engle, Paul. *Chicago Sunday Tribune*, 12 May 1957, p. 3.

54. Hayes, E. Nelson. "Recent Fiction." *The Progressive* 21 (June 1957): 38.

55. Hogan, William. *San Francisco Chronicle*, 22 May 1957, p. 23.

56. Hough, Graham. "New Novels." *Encounter* 10 (February 1958): 84-87.

57. Light, James F. "Nathanael West." *Prairie Schooner* 31 (Fall 1957): 279-283.

58. Peden, William. "Nathanael West." *Virginia Quarterly Review* 33 (Summer 1957): 468-472.

59. Podhoretz, Norman. "A Particular Kind of Joking." *The New Yorker* 33 (18 May 1957): 144-153. [Reprinted, revised, in *Doings and Undoings: The Fifties and After in American Writing*, pp. 66-75; and in Jay Martin, editor, *Nathanael West: A Collection of Critical Essays*, pp. 154-160.]

60. Pritchett, V. S. "*Miss Lonelyhearts.*" *The New Statesman* 54 (7 December 1957): 791-792. [Reprinted, revised, in *The Living Novel & Later Appreciations*, pp. 276-282.]

61. Quinton, Anthony. "Book Reviews." *London Magazine*
5 (May 1958): 72-75.

62. Raven, Simon. "Sub-Men and Super Women."
The Spectator 199 (6 December 1957): 810.

63. Ribalow, Harold U. *Chicago Jewish Forum* 19 (Spring
1961): 251-252.

64. Russell, Ralph. "He Might Have Been a Major Novelist."
Reporter 16 (30 May 1957): 45-46.

65. Schoenwald, Richard L. "No Second Act." *The
Commonweal* 66 (10 May 1957): 162-163.

66. Seymour-Smith, Martin. "Prophet of Black Humour."
The Spectator 221 (19 July 1968): 94-95.

67. Smith, Roger H. "SR's Spotlight on Fiction: 'The
Complete Works of Nathanael West.' " *Saturday Review*
40 (11 May 1957): 13-14. [Portrait on the front cover,
and a biographical note by Archibald Van Voorhees
on p. 13.]

68. White, William. "Belated Fame." *Detroit Free Press*,
26 May 1957, p. C-5.

69. W[illiams], D[avid]. "Mass Living." *The Manchester
Guardian Weekly* 77 (19 December 1957): 10.
[Also reviewed in *The Manchester Guardian*, 3
December 1957, p. 4.]

70. Unsigned. "Rubbing Off the Sheen." *Newsweek* 49
(13 May 1957): 126-127. [Portrait.]

71. ———. "The Great Despiser." *Time* 69 (17 June
1957): 102-105. [Portrait.]

72. ———. "Is a Nathanael West Revival Under Way?"
College English 18 (May 1957): 430. [A note on
The New York Times announcement of *The Complete
Works* and James F. Light's *American Quarterly* article.]

73. ———. *Virginia Kirkus Bookshop Service* 25
(1 March 1957): 194.

Howard Teichmann, *Miss Lonelyhearts* (1957)

74. Hays, Richard. "Dear Miss Lonelyhearts." *The
Commonweal* 67 (25 October 1957): 98.

75. Popkin, Henry. "The Taming of Nathanael West."
The New Republic 137 (21 October 1957): 19-20.

James F. Light, *Nathanael West: An Interpretative Study* (1961)

76. Ashmead, John. *American Literature* 34 (May 1962):
299-300.

77. B., V. A. "The Bizarre Mr. West." *The Chicago Daily
News*, 3 June 1961.

78. Bellman, Samuel I. "Nathanael West's Bitter Life of
Cynicism, Failure Analyzed." *Los Angeles Times*,
13 August 1961, Section C, p. 8.

104

79. Conroy, Jack. "Nightmare World of Nathanael West." *Chicago Sun-Times*, 13 August 1961.

80. Gorn, Lester. "World of West." *San Francisco Examiner*, 9 June 1961.

81. Lid, R. W. *San Francisco Chronicle*, 23 July, 1961, p. 20.

82. Wermuth, Paul C. *Library Journal* 86 (15 September 1961): 2946.

83. White, William. "Nathanael West." *American Book Collector* 12 (October 1961): 4.

84. ———. *Bulletin of Bibliography* 23 (September-December 1961): 126.

85. Unsigned. *Antiquarian Bookman* 28 (7 August 1961): 459.

86. ———. *Virginia Quarterly Review* 37 (Autumn 1961): cxxxvi.

Stanley Edgar Hyman, *Nathanael West* (1962)

87. White, William. "Nathanael West-iana." *American Book Collector* 13 (February 1963): 7.

Victor Comerchero, *Nathanael West: The Ironic Prophet* (1964)

88. Bernard, Kenneth. *Western Humanities Review* 20 (Spring 1966): 170-171.

89. Davis, Robert Murray. *Books Abroad* 39 (Autumn 1965): 452.

90. Lancour, Harold. *Library Journal* 90 (1 February 1965): 648.

91. Lee, Brian. *Notes and Queries* n.s. 17 (February 1970): 79-80.

92. Light, James F. *American Literature* 37 (May 1965): 222-223.

93. Ruhe, Edward L. *Midcontinent American Studies Journal* 7 (1966): 61-63.

94. Stafford, William T. In James Woodress, editor, *American Literary Scholarship: An Annual / 1964*, Durham, North Carolina: Duke University Press, 1966, p. 178.

Randall Reid, *The Fiction of Nathanael West* (1967)

95. Bush, Clive. *Journal of American Studies* 3 (July 1969): 157-158.

96. Eisinger, Chester E. *English Language Notes* 6 (December 1968): 148-151.

97. French, Warren. In James Woodress, editor, *American Literary Scholarship: An Annual / 1967*, Durham, North Carolina: Duke University Press, 1969, pp. 184-185. [See also "The Cosmogonists," pp. 183-187.]

98. Gado, Frank. *Studia Neophilologica* 41 (1969): 203-204.

99. Green, James L. *American Literature Abstracts* 2 (1969): 339-341.

100. Gross, Barry. *Studies in the Novel* 1 (Fall 1969): 377-378.

101. Hicks, Granville. "Academe's Blue Chip Authors." *Saturday Review* 51 (22 June 1968): 25.

102. Janssens, G. A. M. *Neophilologus* 53 (1969): 238-239.

103. Jones, Joel M. *American Literary Realism, 1870-1910* 4 (1968): 94-96.

104. Lee, Brian. *Notes and Queries* n.s. 17 (February 1970): 79-80.

105. Light, James F. *American Literature* 40 (November 1968): 421-422.

106. Lund, Mary Graham. *Per / Se* 3 (1968): 79.

107. Pops, Martin. *Criticism* 10 (Fall 1968): 367-370.

108. Raines, C. A. *Library Journal* 93 (1 February 1968): 554.

109. White, William. " 'Go West!' Notes from a Bibliographer." *American Book Collector* 19 (January 1969): 7-10.

110. Unsigned. *Choice* 5 (July 1968): 626.

111. ———. *Prairie Schooner* 42 (Winter 1968 / 69): 365.

112. ———. *Virginia Quarterly Review* 44 (Summer 1968): cxiii.

Jay Martin, *Nathanael West: The Art of His Life* (1970)

113. Adelman, Maurice, Jr. *America* 123 (28 November
1970): 467.

114. Bedient, Calvin. "In Dreams Begin." *Partisan Review* 38
(1971): 345-349.

115. Bell, Martin. "A Hard Life." *Encounter* 37
(September 1971): 78.

116. Cassill, R. V. "The Dossier on Nathanael West."
Chicago Tribune Book World 4 (5 July 1970): 3.
[Portrait.]

117. Darrach, Brad. "A Great Despiser." *Time* 96 (17 August
1970): 64-65. [Portrait.]

118. Dupee, F. W. "Doing West." *The New York Review of
Books* 15 (24 September 1970): 10-12. [Drawing of
West by David Levine.]

119. French, Philip. "Locust Years." *New Statesman* 81
(14 May 1971): 673-674.

120. French, Warren. In J. Albert Robbins, editor, *American
Literary Scholarship: An Annual / 1970*, Durham,
North Carolina: Duke University Press, 1972, pp. 245-246.

121. Gado, Frank. *American Literature* 43 (May 1971):
298-299.

122. Giannone, Richard. "Freaks, Con Men, Hustlers."
The Nation 211 (17 August 1970): 120-122.

123. Howe, Irving. "That Rare and Marvelous Figure—
An Original." *New York Times Book Review*, 12 July
1970, Section 7, pp. 1, 40. [Portrait.]

124. Hyman, Stanley Edgar. "Prince Myshkin in Hollywood."
The New Leader 53 (11 May 1970) : 6-7.

125. Kennedy, William. "Sad Tales Dot the Career of
Nathanael West." *The National Observer*,
13 July 1970, p. 19.

126. Lehmann-Haupt, Christopher. "If You Love West's Art,
You'll Like His Life." *New York Times*, 15 June 1970,
p. 41.

127. Light, James F. *Satire Newsletter* 8 (Fall 1970) : 65-68.

128. Malin, Irving. "Late to Honor." *The Catholic World*
212 (November 1970) : 110.

129. Maloff, Saul. "Beware of 'Literature Boys'!" *The
Commonweal* 93 (23 October 1970) : 96-98.

130. McCormick, Jay. "The Nathanael West Story: About a
Man That Time Doublecrossed." *The [Detroit] Sunday
News*, 12 July 1970, Section E, p. 5.

131. Oberbeck, S. K. "Disaster Fascinated Him." *Newsweek*
75 (29 June 1970) : 80-81. [Portrait.]

132. Rascoe, Judith. "A Writer Wrapped in Questions."
The Christian Science Monitor, 30 July 1970, p. 5.
[Portrait.]

133. Samuels, Charles Thomas. "Suicide as Rhetoric."
The New Republic 162 (23 May 1970) : 23-24.

134. Samsell, R. L. *Fitzgerald / Hemingway Annual* [3] (1971): 351-357.

135. Schorer, Mark. "Nathan Weinstein: The Cheated." *The Atlantic* 226 (October 1970): 127-130.

136. Sissman, L. E. "West." *The New Yorker* 46 (10 October 1970): 185-190.

137. Swados, Harvey. *Saturday Review* 53 (27 June 1970): 28-29. [Portrait.]

138. Wakefield, Dan. "Mister Lonelyhearts." *The American Scholar* 39 (Summer 1970): 524-526.

139. White, William. "A Full Account of the Sources of Nathanael West's Genius." *Library Journal* 95 (1 June 1970): 2160.

140. Unsigned. *Choice* 7 (December 1970): 1376.

141. ————. "A Knocker in a World of Boosters." *Times Literary Supplement*, 10 September 1971, p. 1080.

David Madden, editor. *The Cheaters and the Cheated* (1973)

142. Martin, Jay. *American Literature* 46 (November 1974): 410-411.

143. White, William. "Not Just Murder: Books, Sex, and West." *Presenting Moonshine* 2 (December 1974): 3-5.

V. Theses and Dissertations

1. Brand, John Michael, III. *Fiction as Decreation: The Novels of Nathanel West.* Fort Worth, Texas: Texas Christian University, 1969. 215 pp. [Ph.D. dissertation. See *Dissertation Abstracts International* 30 (February 1970):3449-A.]

2. Briggs, Arlen John. *Nathanael West and Surrealism.* Eugene: University of Oregon, 1972. 237 pp. [Ph.D. dissertation. See *Dissertation Abstracts International* 33 (June 1973): 6901-A-6902-A.]

3. Brown, Daniel Russell. *Nathanael West: The War Within.* Detroit: Wayne State University, 1969. 189 pp. [Ph.D. dissertation. See *Dissertation Abstracts International* 32 (November 1971): 2676-A.]

4. Comerchero, Victor. *Nathanael West: The Tuning Fork.* Iowa City: State University of Iowa, 1961. 248 pp. [Ph.D. dissertation. See *Dissertation Abstracts* 22 (1962): 2791. Published, revised, as a book.]

5. Cramer, Carter M. *The World of Nathanael West: A Critical Interpretation.* Emporia: Kansas State Teachers College, 1971. [M.A. thesis. Published, revised, as a pamphlet.]

5a. Frizot, Daniel Marie Louis. *The Clown Figure in Louis-Fernand Céline and Nathanael West, or the Tragi-comic in Modern Fiction.* Lafayette, Indiana: Purdue University,

1973. 252pp. [Ph.D. dissertation. See *Dissertation Abstracts International* 34 (March 1974): 5908-A-5909-A.]

6. Goldsmith, Lynne. *Nathanael West's "Miss Lonelyhearts" and "The Day of the Locust": "Over Everything a Funeral Hush."* Rochester, Michigan: Oakland University, 1970. 28 pp. [M.A. thesis.]

7. Houston, James D. *Three Varieties of Grotesquerie in Twentieth Century American Fiction.* Stanford, California: Stanford University, 1962. [M.A. thesis.]

7a. Keyes, John. *Nathanael West: A Technical View.* Toronto: University of Toronto, 1972. [Ph.D. dissertation.]

8. Levart, Herman H. *Nathanael West: A Study of His Fiction.* New York: Columbia University, 1952. 58 pp. [M.A. thesis.]

9. Light, James F. *Nathanael West: A Critical Study, With Some Biographical Material.* Syracuse: Syracuse University, 1953. viii, 255 pp. [Ph.D. dissertation. Published, revised, as a book.]

10. Locklin, Gerald Ivan. *A Critical Study of the Novels of Nathanael West.* Tucson: University of Arizona, 1964. 301 pp. [Ph.D. dissertation. See *Dissertation Abstracts* 25 (December 1964): 3576-3577.]

11. Lorch, Thomas M. *The Peculiar Half-World of Nathanael West.* New Haven: Yale University, 1964. 269 pp. [Ph.D. dissertation. See *Dissertation Abstracts* 26 (October 1965): 2218.]

12. Mann, Nora Jeannette Williams. *The Novels of Nathanael West*. Columbia: University of Missouri, 1968. 181 pp. [Ph.D. dissertation. See *Dissertation Abstracts* 29 (February 1969): 2716-A.]

13. Michaels, I. Lloyd. *A Particular Kind of Joking: Nathanael West and Burlesque*. Buffalo: State University of New York at Buffalo, 1972. 191 pp. [Ph.D. dissertation. See *Dissertation Abstracts International* 33 (1973): 5188-A-5189-A.]

14. Petrullo, Helen Batchelor. *Satire and Freedom: Sinclair Lewis, Nathanael West, and James Thurber*. Syracuse: Syracuse University, 1967. 219 pp. [Ph.D. dissertation. See *Dissertation Abstracts* 28 (October 1967): 1445-A.]

15. Pisk, George Michael. *A Fire in Dreamland: A Suggested Unifying Principle in the Works of Nathanael West*. Austin: University of Texas, 1959. 134 pp. [M.A. thesis.]

16. Reid, Randall Clyde. *Nathanael West: No Redeemer, No Promised Land*. Stanford, California: Stanford University, 1967. 208 pp. [Ph.D. dissertation. See *Dissertation Abstracts* 27 (January 1967): 2159-A. Published, revised, as a book.]

17. Robinson, David Edgar. *Unaccomodated Man: The Estranged World in Contemporary American Fiction*. Durham, North Carolina: Duke University, 1971. 297 pp. [Ph.D. dissertation. See *Dissertation Abstracts International* 32 (April 1972); 5803-A-5804-A.]

18. Schneider, Cyril M. *Nathanael West: A Study of His Work*. New York: New York University, 1953. 74 pp. [M.A. thesis.]

19. Smith, Marcus Ayres Joseph, Jr. *The Art and Influence of Nathanael West.* Madison: University of Wisconsin, 1964. 318 pp. [Ph.D. dissertation. See *Dissertation Abstracts* 25 (January 1965): 4155-4156.]

20. Wadlington, Warwick Paul. *The Theme of the Confidence Game in Certain Major American Writers.* New Orleans, Louisiana: Tulane University, 1967. 268 pp. [Ph.D. dissertation. See *Dissertation Abstracts* 28 (March 1968): 3691-A.]

21. Wexelblatt, Robert Bernard. *Disintegration in the Works of F. Scott Fitzgerald and Nathanael West.* Waltham, Massachusetts: Brandeis University, 1973. 294 pp. [Ph.D. dissertation. See *Dissertation Abstracts International* 34 (January 1974): 4296-A.]

22. Zlotnick, Joan C. *Nathanael West: A Study of the Paradox of Art.* New York: New York University, 1969. 148 pp. [Ph.D. dissertation. See *Dissertation Abstracts International* 30 (February 1970): 3482-A-3483-A.]

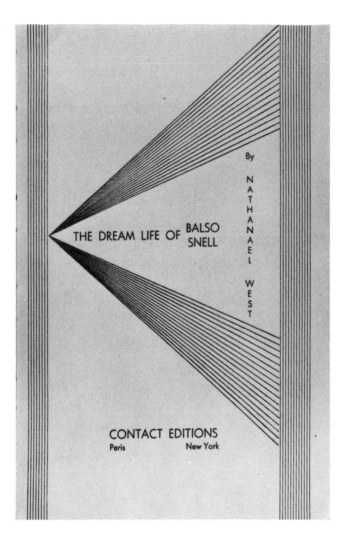

THE DREAM LIFE OF BALSO SNELL

By NATHANAEL WEST

CONTACT EDITIONS

Paris   New York

MISS LONELYHEARTS

by Nathanael West

LIVERIGHT · INC · PUBLISHERS

NEW YORK

A COOL
MILLION

The Dismantling of Lemuel Pitkin

BY

NATHANAEL WEST

COVICI · FRIEDE · *Publishers*

NEW YORK

Nathanael West

THE DAY
OF THE
LOCUST

Random House, New York

Appendix: Uncollected Writings of Nathanael West

Rondeau

My lady's eyes appear to be
Like brimming pools of ecstasy,
Deep wells, from which the twinkles flow
Unceasingly as on they go
To charm me with their witchery;
Mayhap an easy prey they see,
Enmeshed by their dexterity;
I can't protest; they thrill me so—
My lady's eyes.

Although they gaze alluringly,
Appealing with such potentcy,
Oft times in them I see a glow
Which warns me that I should go slow,
For then, you know, I really see
My lady lies!

The Brown Jug
Jugful No. 2, p. 24
December 1922

Euripides—A Playwright

The tawdry melodrama of "Uncle Tom's Cabin." The dirt
of a Restoration play by Wycherley. The sex alarums by the
propagandist Brieux. The bloody sensationalism of the Old
Testament. The box-office symbolisms of Carl Capek. The
waving of his country's flag as George M. Cohan never waved it.
The stretching of the long arm of coincidence as Thomas
Hardy never dared stretch it. The eternal triangle. In short,
the art of that great Greek dramatist, Euripides.

Euripides is a perambulating source-book and a consistent
fount of inspiration for the genius of all subsequent civilizations.
Seneca, Dante, Racine, Corneille, Goethe, Grilplatzer, Milton,
Keats, Shelley, Browning (their names are as the Egyptian
Gods in number) all are in deep debt to him. Even Shakespeare
has the master player in Hamlet do a poor version of Hecuba
to prove his merit. Being able to quote Euripides has saved
not alone the first-nighters, who were in the Sicilian expedition,
but also many a latter-day intellectual has good cause to burn
offerings of thanks at his shrine. The peculiar fact about
this wholesale borrowing and rewriting of Euripides is,
that no matter how great the genius of the subsequent writer,
he invariably fails. Euripides, to explain this, might paraphrase
Shakespeare and say, "He who steals my ideas steals
something as cheap as potatoes in Ireland, while he who
steals my style steals my very essence." This seems rational
and adequate explanation of Seneca's magnificent failures and
Henri Bernstein's cheap plagiarisms.

To turn to a more particular criticism of Euripides' plays
in the "Alcestis," Euripides wrote one of the best of plays,
full of true pathos and keen humor, both of which sometimes
verge upon burlesque. The happy ending is understood from

the start and none of the grief is sentimental. This is the play which J. J. Chapman says, "The bourgeoisie takes his half-grown family to see."

Heracles struts, waves his club and shows his biceps; the women wail, Admetus whines; there is grace, there is spice— there are laughs and there are tears. And there is a happy ending that everybody knows is coming but in which he delights, nevertheless. Alcestis returns and is accepted mid speeches which God might quote. No painting by Vermeer has half its happy loveliness or one by Gaugin its color. It is a play that Lewis Carroll's Alice must see in her looking glass.

To Milton and to Swinburne a Greek play is a symphony of beautiful, solemn declamation and ceremony. To me, however, it is more—it is exciting, varied, and moving life, in which every word sparkles with action and every action with wit. "In seeking to understand Greek plays we must forget Milton and think rather of Molière," says James Huneker. This is what we must keep in mind when we read the "Bacchae." Most of the students of this play make it out to be a mystical allegory or a sort of Oberammergau play. Apropos of this, I. T. Beckwith, in preface to the "Bacchae" says, "A play in which faith celebrates its rights, and unbelief is put to shame, must, by reason of the seriousness of its import and the lofty religious inspiration pervading the whole and manifesting itself in many brilliant and profound utterances, have attained great fame in antiquity." It was much read, as the frequent citations and reminiscences of the Greek and Roman writers show, and was often cited.

"The choral odes follow the progress of the action more closely, perhaps, than in any other play of Euripides, expressing the emotions that accompany a devout faith as it passes from the most buoyant hopefulness through a gradual darkening struggle out again into complete triumph."

Let us now examine the text of the "Bacchae." According to the legend, the Bacchantes, followers of Dionysus, tore Pentheus to pieces for his refusal to worship the new god. Both Pentheus and Dionysus are the grandsons of Cadmus, one of the Argonauts. At the time the story begins, Cadmus had resigned the government of Thebes, and turned it over to his grandson, Pentheus.

At the opening of the play Dionysus enters as prologue and explains that he has come disguised as a mortal with the Bacchantes in his train. He says that he has come back to his birthplace in order to punish his mother's two sisters, who have never taken seriously the story of his divine birth. Thebes soon discovers that Dionysus is a god.

Next comes a vaudeville act that is one of the finest things ever done on the stage. The team is Tiresias, the mythical sooth-sayer, and Cadmus, the great mythic Hellene. James Huneker calls these old men Moses and Aaron. They come in, dressed for Bacchic rites, each with a small thyrsus in his hands, and garlands of flowers on their heads, "beribboned for the fray"—Chapman has a good description of their "act" in his "Greek Genius," in which he says, "They exhibit the characters of the gay old bourgeoisie, delighted at their own temerity, knowing they will be laughed at, yet resolved to enjoy themselves." . . . The audience must have gripped its umbrellas with joy! . . . The old darlings enter, meeting as by appointment, clap each other on the shoulder, admire each others dresses, swear they will dance like good ones—they alone of the city. But they alone are wise! "They will not be ashamed of their old age, not they! The god never distinguishes between old and young, but demands worship from both: they clasp hands in rapture (Tiresias being blind) and are about to leave when enters the gloomy and boorish Pentheus.

As a foil to the old gentlemen, Pentheus is perfect." This
scene of the two old men belongs among the greatest things
in drama.

The chorus, after their departure, celebrates in a hymn
to Bacchus and Venus. This hymn is in a manner that P.
Descharme thinks sublimely religious, and A. W. Verral a
ribald drinking song. But it is not a drinking song, Chapman
thinks, or a religious hymnal. It is as refined as Praxitiles'
statuary and as conventional. All I will venture is that it is
very good poetry.

There is hardly a page in this play where the Greek fear
of being laughed at does not come up. When Dionysus tells of
his triumph over Pentheus in the stable, the punishment of
Pentheus is made drastic because of the ridicule to which it
makes him subject. (Even Medea kills her children
out of the fear that she will be ridiculed for her lack of
success in life.) I cannot continue to tell in detail the rest of
the play, but you cannot touch it anywhere without having
the desire, when once started, to write and never stop writing.
There is not a moment in the whole play where it is not
dynamic and stimulating.

In summing up, I feel the desire to express the unexpressible
praise, but I realize that I am incapable. The most I can
accomplish is to throw a few soiled flowers on a Parnassus
of laurel and bay, heaped up by his more capable admirers.

In reading Euripides, we find ourselves ready to classify him
at moments as a satirist and at other moments as a man of
feeling. Of course he was both. Sometimes he seems like a
religious man and again like a charlatan. Of course he was
neither. He was a great playwright.

Casements
Vol. 1, pp. [2-4]
July 1923

Death

Cherished inspirer of minor poets,
How many adolescent wails
Have reached your fleshless ears!
Shall I join that inane chorus
With my poor echo of an old cry?
Scold you for a thief,
Cherish you as a friend,
Beg you for more days,
Or vainly dare you take me?
Why must you disturb
The mediocre mind to thought
And scare small souls to God?

Casements
Vol. 2, p. 15
May 1924

A Barefaced Lie

With my dunnage at my feet, I stood on the porch of the
Circle City Hotel waiting for the stage. I had been advised
by my friend, Red Patterson, the gum booter, to ride only with
Boulder Bill—and to listen politely to all he had to say.

Presently a team, with buckboard, turned the corner below
and came up to the hotel porch at a brisk trot. As the driver
pulled the horses up sharply and set the brake I had a good
look at Boulder Bill. He was a huge, thick-set, active-appearing
man. His face was tanned, his mouth completely covered
by a heavy, sandy moustache. He wrapped the lines around
the brake staff and sprang lightly over the wheel onto the porch.

As he advanced he fixed me with a steady stare from his keen gray eyes.

"Morning, Stranger," he called, "bound up the river?" I involuntarily gave back a step, for of all the voices given to man, Boulder Bill's voice was certainly one of the strongest. I recovered myself and said that I would like to go up to the upper camp.

"You're just same as there, pardner," bellowed Boulder, "for when old Boulder Bill starts out he always gets in."

"Just look at that team of horses," his voice sank to a whisper that was audible a block away. "See the one on the near side, that's a Circle H horse, and anybody'll tell you that when you see a Circle H horse you're looking at a horse."

Bill's face was beaming by this time, and he gave my arm a violent squeeze.

He moved about quickly and methodically, loading the baggage and mail, all the while keeping up a loud conversation. I stepped over to get on the stage when I heard a sort of snort from Boulder Bill. I looked around and he was staring balefully at a young fellow who had just come out of the hotel carrying a dunnage bag.

The young man was a very pleasant-faced chap and appeared to be in the best of humor.

"I'll go with you up to the lower camp," he said to Bill.

Boulder Bill's face was a study as he continued to stare at the passenger. Disgust, anger, and outraged pride mingled in his expression. He turned and motioned to me with his thumb to take the front seat, and said, "Set up there, Stranger, anybody can see *you* are a white man."

The other passenger, with a grin, climbed into the rear seat, and Bill, after another prolonged stare and a contemptuous snort mounted the stage and in a noticeable silence, drove off.

I was mystified. There seemed nothing in the appearance or conduct of my fellow passenger to warrant this treatment.

It was soon apparent that Bill was an experienced driver. He urged the team along at a fast trot. He was evidently gripped by strong emotions for he stared straight ahead and maintained a stony silence broken only by his occasional snort. At intervals he would exclaim, under his breath, "Liar!" "Humpf!" *"Liars!"*

At the lower camp he did not get down from the stage. He tossed out the mail and he did not look as the other passenger alighted, nor respond when he called out a pleasant good-bye to us.

After we had proceeded a short distance from the lower camp Boulder Bill suddenly turned and fixed me with a steady stare. Then he burst out, "Stranger, as man to man, what do you think of liars? Hold on now, I don't mean honest liars or liars that have to do it, but just low-down bare-faced ornery skunk liars. Liars that just tell a downright bare-faced lie just to get somebody laughed at.

"That's the kind of liars what I mean."

I was taken aback by his vehemence, but managed to state that to me all liars were objectionable.

"Now pardner," went on Boulder Bill, "there is different kinds of liars, some lie to hurt, some lie for fun, but the lowest down kind is the kind that just tell a lie that don't do themselves no good, but just get other folks laughed at. That's the kind of a liar what that Yahoo is what just got off at the lower camp."

I expressed my astonishment and said that the passenger looked like a decent chap.

"Right there is where you're fooled, Stranger, that low-down ornery skunk is the most bare-faced, mean, siwash liar that ever hit the country, and I can prove it to you. Why, last fall

I was at the upper camp and was packing out the trail to the post.
You know, I am a rustler, pardner, and away before breakfast
I was out in the corral putting on the packsaddles and fixing
the tie ropes so that after we got our feed we could go
right out and start lashing the packs on.

"Big Pete and I had nine mules, and I would ketch a mule
and cinch on the packsaddle and then turn him loose and
get another. It was away before daylight, and I kept on until
I had used up my nine packsaddles. When I started to go
out of the corral I run against a mule what didn't have a
packsaddle on. That was darned funny, pardner, for when
I cinch a mule he stays cinched, and I knowed I didn't put no
two packsaddles on the same mule. I was looking around
to see what was up when I see a mule near me climbing the
fence like a dog does!

"Now, Stranger, anybody can tell you that a mule is a
curious critter, but climbing a fence like a dog does is too much.
I just aimed to amble over and grab that mule by the tail and
pull him back and kick the stuffing out of him. I made a
swipe at his tail, but Stranger, you can burn me for a dead
sinner if there was any tail there. Before I could get on my
balance again he gave a little flip and slapped me in the face
with his hind leg as he went over.

"And, pardner, what do you think it was? A darned fool
bear!"

Bill paused with his narrative, and gave me a prolonged,
steady stare.

"Now, everybody," he went on, "knows that bears have
funny points, but being in there with the mules was a
queer proposition. Whether he was lonesome or just happened
in nobody can tell, and of course, in the dark I just put a
saddle on him like anybody would. After we got back from
the Post I was down in the saloon and just happened
to tell about it.

"Now, pardner, there is nothing wrong with that story. It could happen to me, or it could happen to you, or it could happen to anybody. There was the bear and there was the packsaddle gone.

"The boys all listened decently, and then talked it over. Old Josh Speaks said he heard tell of a similar story over in the Caribou once, but he did not set much store by it then, but if it happened right in camp it must be all right.

"I told the boys all to come up and have a drink, and as we fronted the bar that big-mouthed Yahoo what just got off at the lower camp slapped his hand down on the bar, and started on a regular hyena laugh, and said, "That explains it." Of course we all stopped for him to have his say, and, pardner, what do you think he told? Of all the bare-faced wild-eyed—humpf!"

Bill stopped completely out of breath; he struggled for air for a minute, and recovering himself, went on:

"The low-down siwash said he was coming down by Fish Point that day, and he heard some kind of a ruckus going on over by the river bank, and, looking over, what did we expect he saw? He said there was an old bear standing on a stump grunting and jabbering away like he was the boss of things, and there was two more bears down on the bar a-packing a load of salmon on another bear what had a packsaddle on, and two more bears still was catching salmon and carrying them up to the packyard; and there was a trail up the bank to a *cache* up on the hill.

"Of course, everybody's eyes bulged out, mine more than anybody's. Of all the wild-eyed lies, how in the world could anybody expect a bear to throw a diamond or even a squaw hitch?

"Well, we all looked at each other just goggled-eyed. When old Josh Speaks had his wiskey about half down

he snorted right out and got choked. And everybody began
to pound each other on the back, and just gave him the
horse laugh.

"After we had quieted down some of the boys began to
look at me in a funny way and snicker. And, of course,
I went home to my cabin and I ain't been back since."

Boulder Bill's face got redder and redder, and his voice
rose to a mighty roar: "Of all the low-down, bare, bare."
His voice broke, and ended in a faint whisper, "bare-faced
bear lies, pardner—bear-faced bear lies. . ."

Overland Monthly
Vol. 87, pp. 210, 219
July 1929

"Through the Hole in the Mundane Millstone"

Three men read *The Dream Life of Balso Snell* and, having
in mind perhaps an older story involving Picasso, exclaimed
in rapid succession:

"Almost as funny as the Venus de Milo!"

"As funny as the Venus de Milo!"

"Funnier than the Venus de Milo!"

We quote this incident not only because the book is extremely
funny, but also because the hero of it, Balso Snell, a lyric poet
by trade, often indulges in violent exclamations. The examples
that follow have been chosen at random from the text:

"O Anon! O Onan!"

"O Beer! O Meyerbeer! O Bach! O Offenbach!"

"O Constipation of Desire! O Diarrhoea of Love!"

English humor has always prided itself on being good natured and in the best of taste. This fact makes it difficult to compare N. W. West with other comic writers, as he is vicious, mean, ugly, obscene and insane. We feel with good cause. For much too long has the whimsical, family-joke (tongue in cheek, hand over heart, good-fellows all) dominated our literature. With the French, however, West can well be compared. In his use of the violently disassociated, the dehumanized marvelous, the deliberately criminal and imbecilic, he is much like Guillaume Apollinaire, Jarry, Ribemont-Dessaignes, Raymond Roussel, and certain of the surrealistes.

Nevertheless, the mechanism used—an "anywhere out of the world" device—makes a formal comparison with Lewis Carroll possible. Just as Alice escapes through the looking glass, Balso Snell escapes the real world by entering the Wooden Horse of the Greeks which he finds in the tall grass surrounding the walls of Troy. Inside he hires a philosophic guide who insists on discussing the nature of art. After a violent argument, Balso eludes him only to run into Maloney the Areopagite who is attempting to crucify himself with thumb tacks. Maloney tells Balso that he is writing a life of Saint Puce. This saint is a flea who built a church in the armpit of our Lord; a church "whose walls are the flesh of Christ, whose windows are rose with the blood of Christ." After Maloney, he meets John Raskolnikov Gilson, the twelve year old murderer of an idiot, and Miss McGeeney, a school teacher who is writing the life of Samuel Perkins, a man who can smell the strength of iron or even the principles involved in an isosceles triangle.

It becomes apparent to Balso that the intestine of the horse is inhabited solely by authors in search of an audience. Disgusted, he attempts to get out but is tricked into listening to other tales. All of these tales are elephantine close-ups of various

literary positions and their technical methods; close-ups
that make Kurt Schwitters' definition, "Tout ce'que l'artiste
crache, c'est l'art" seem like an understatement.

Advertisement for
The Dream Life of Balso Snell
(New York: Moss and Kamin, 1931)

Book Marks for Today

We have had some experience with the little magazine
and think that such a statement as the one recently made by
Mr. Frank Shay in connection with Contempo ought not
to pass unchallenged.

When he wrote about "panhandling magazines," he was
taking a crack at one of the few decent things in American
letters. Apparently he is unacquainted with their sponsors and
ignorant of the purpose they serve.

As to the sponsors, it would be hard to find greater idealists
in the literary world. Invariably they have spent money and
given time to what they knew from the start was to be a
losing venture. As to purpose, the little magazine in the past
has found audiences for such writers as Sherwood Anderson,
Ben Hecht, Ernest Hemingway (Little Review); Robert Coates,
Malcolm Cowley, Allen Tate, Hart Crane (Transition);
Ruth Suckow, Edna Ferber, Glenway Westcott (The
Midland)—to mention but a few.

Surely the unpaid writer for that type of magazine has little
to complain of, since he and "litrachoor"—but never the
sponsors—get anything out of it.

(With Julian L. Shapiro)
New York World-Telegram
20 October 1931, p. 23

Miss Lonelyhearts and the Lamb

After a cold morning and a rainy afternoon, the evening had turned warm. Thomas Matlock, the Miss Lonelyhearts of the New York Evening Hawk (Are you in trouble? Do you need advice? Write to Miss Lonelyhearts and she will help you), decided to walk from the Hawk Building across the park to Delehanty's speakeasy. He entered the North Gate and swallowed large mouthfulls of the heavy shadow that curtained its opening. He walked into the shadow of a lamp post that lay on the path like a spear, and like a spear it pierced him through.

Yesterday's snow had turned to black slush and the air smelt as though it had been artificially heated. Surprised by the unexpected warmth, Matlock carefully examined the mottled ground for signs of spring. He was unable to discover any. The decay covering its surface was not the decay in which life generates.

Last year, he remembered, the dynamite of May had failed to quicken these soiled fields. It had taken all the brutality of summer to torture a few green spikes through the exhausted dirt.

What the little park needed, even more than he did, was a drink. Tomorrow he would ask Broken-hearted, Sick-of-it-all, Bird-in-a-gilded-cage, Unfortunate-cripple, Disillusioned-with-tubercular-husband, and the rest of his correspondents to come here and water the soil with their tears. Flowers would then spring up, flowers that smelled of feet.

"Ah, humanity . . .["] But his gloom was too profound for him to escape so easily. "Ah, humanity . . ." The joke went into a dying fall. He tried to break its fall by laughing at himself.

But why, when Shrike was waiting at Delehanty's to do a much better job? "Matlock, my friend, I advise you to give your readers stones. When they ask for bread don't give them crackers as does the church, don't, like the state, tell them to eat cake. Explain that man cannot live on bread alone and give them stones. Teach them to pray for their daily stone: Give us this day our daily stone."

Matlock had given the readers of his column many stones—suffering is good for the soul; the meek shall inherit the earth; laugh and the world laughs with you; the simple joys are the best—but he could not give them the stone that had formed in his gut, and it was the only stone he had left.

He sat down on a bench. His heart was an overdrawn bow that must shoot soon or break. At what? He searched the sky for a target. Nothing less than a celestial shooting gallery would do. But the grey sky looked as if it had been rubbed with a soiled eraser. It held no angels, flaming crosses, olive-bearing doves, wheels within wheels; there was only a newspaper that struggled in the air like a kite with a broken spine.

He decided against Delehanty's and started home. He did not want to listen to Shrike who had discovered that he still worried about Christ and for his benefit had invented a new church, The First Church of Christ Dentist, and a new trinity, the Father, Son and Wire-haired Fox Terrier. Shrike and his stage, the speakeasy, made him feel that he was wandering, lost without hope of escape, among the scenery and costumes in the cellar of an ancient theatre.

His room was furnished with a bed, a table, and two chairs. The walls were bare except for a mirror and an ivory Christ. He had removed the cross to which the figure had been delicately fastened with tiny silver nails and had spiked it to the wall.

But the desired effect had not been obtained. It did not writhe; it remained calmly decorative.

Matlock was very tired. Before undressing, however, he examined himself in the mirror. Although his cheap clothes had too much style, he still looked like the son of a small town Baptist minister. In a few years he would look like his father the minister. A beard would become him, he judged, would accent the old-testament look. But even without a beard no one could fail to recognize the New England man of God. He smiled. The Susan Chesters, the Beatrice Fairfaxs, the Miss Lonelyhearts are the priests of twentieth century America.

He took a cigarette and the Modern Library edition of the Brothers Karamazov to bed with him. The marker was in the chapter containing the sermons of Father Zosima.

"Love a man even in his sin, for that is the semblance of Divine Love and is the highest love on earth. Love all God's creation, the whole and every grain of sand in it. Love the animals, love the plants, love everything. If you love everything, you will perceive the divine mystery in things. Once you perceive it, you will begin to comprehend it better every day. And you will come at last to love the whole world with an all-embracing love." . . .

It was pleasant in bed and the cigarette tasted good. He was a fool for letting Shrike and the letters get him down. The way to do it was to take things easy. Laugh at Shrike's jokes when they were amusing and walk away from him when they are not. The same with the letters. Do ones best to help by giving practical advice about hospitals, lawyers, jobs, even practical advice about God. Try to make things easier for them. And even try to love them. But don't embarrass oneself and them with love. Don't lick lepers.

But he knew that he was incapable of so much humility. His vocation was of a different sort. As a boy in his father's church he had discovered that something began to stir in him when he shouted the name of Christ, something secret and enormous. He had played with this thing, but he never allowed it to come entirely alive. Now, thinking of Christ, he felt this thing stir in him.

He would think ever of Christ and would be humble and full of love. He would answer the letters out of the greatness of his love. His column would be syndicated and his message would be read all over the world. The whole world, through him, would learn to love. The Kingdom of Heaven would arrive . . . He would see Christ's face. . . They would place him next to the lamb. . . .

Matlock fell asleep. He dreamed that he was a little boy in a flannel nightgown, praying with his head on his mother's knees. He loved his mother very much and she loved him. The chair in which his mother sat loved him and he loved the chair. His mother's cool silk dress, the carpet on which he knelt, the wallpaper, the bed, all loved him and he returned their love.

But his mother disappeared and he found himself before a microphone on the platform of a crowded auditorium. In the crowd he recognized Brokenhearted, Sick-of-it-all, Unfortunate-cripple, Bird-in-a-gilded-cage, Disillusioned-with-tubercular-husband and many of his other correspondents. No matter how he struggled his prayer was Shrike's prayer and his voice was the voice of a conductor calling stations.

"Oh Lord, we are not of those who wash in wine, water, urine, vinegar, fire, oil, bay rum, milk, champagne, or boric acid. Oh Lord, we wash solely in the Blood of the Lamb." . . .

He was back in his college dormitory with Steve Garvey and Jud Hume. They had been arguing religion all night. When the whiskey gave out they decided to go to the market for some applejack.

The long walk through the streets of the sleeping town sobered them, but in the bright fields beyond the town their drunk was renewed by the smells of vegetable birth. When they got to the market the stalls were not yet set up and they reeled among the loaded carts. The farmers took their horseplay good naturedly . . . "Boys from the college on a spree."

They found the cider man and brought [bought?] three quarts of hard, then wandered into the section where livestock was sold. A farmer had half a dozen lambs for sale and they stopped to fool with the animals. Jud Hume suggested that they buy one and roast it over a fire in the woods. But it was his idea that they should sacrifice it to God before barbecueing it.

He went to the cutlery stand for a knife, while Jud and Steve bargained for a lamb. When he returned, they bought the youngest, a little, stiff-legged thing, all head, and paraded it through the market into the woods, singing an obscene version of Mary had a little lamb. He marched first, carrying the knife, Jud last, leading the lamb.

In a clearing, on a hill back of the market, they found a large rock. They covered the rock with wild flowers and laid the lamb on the flowers. He was elected priest. While Steve and Jud lurched around the crude altar, he gripped the struggling animal with one hand and with the other, holding up the knife, gestured at the sun.

"Christ. Christ. Jesus Christ," he screamed and bringing the knife down hard made a deep gash in the lamb's neck. Because of its terrible struggles his next stroke went wrong and he broke the knife on the stone altar. Steve and Jud pulled the lamb's head back so that he could saw at its throat, but only a small piece of the blade was left in the handle and he was unable to cut through the matted wool. A thick stream of blood pumped over their heads and clothes.

When the lamb tore from their grasp, they let it go staggering off into the underbrush and broke into a panic-stricken run along the path that led out of the woods. After they had sobered up a little, he tried to get them to go back with him and put the lamb out of its misery, but they refused to go. He went back alone and found it lying under a bush. He crushed its head with a rock and left the carcass to the flies that had settled on the blood-stained altar flowers.

Contact
Vol. 1, pp. 80-85
February 1932

Miss Lonelyhearts and the Dead Pan

Only my leader was finished: "Life *is* worthwhile, for it is full of dreams and peace, gentleness and ecstasy, and faith that burns like a clear white flame on a grim dark altar." Although the dead line was but a few minutes away, I sat watching the rain turn the dusty tar roofs below me into shiny patent leather. I had found it impossible to continue. You can't go on finding the same joke funny thirty times a day for months on end. And on most days I received more than thirty letters, all of them alike, as though stamped from the dough of suffering with a heart-shaped cookie knife.

I turned from the window to re-read Broad-shoulders' letter.

Dear Miss Lonelyhearts—

Being an admirer of your column because you give such good advice to people in trouble as that is what I am in also I would appreciate very much if you can advise me what to do after I tell you my troubles.

138

During the war I was told if I wanted to do my bit I should
marry the man I was engaged to as he was going away
to help Uncle Sam and to make a long story short I was
married to him. After the war was over he still had to remain
in the army for one more year as he signed an agreement
and I went to busines as while doing this patriotic stunt
he had only $18 dollars to his name. I worked for three years
steady and then had to stay home because I became a mother
and in the meantime of those years my husband would get a
job and then he would tire of it or wanted to roam. It was
all right before the baby came because when I was working
bills were paid but when I stopped everything went sliding
backward. Then two years went by and a baby boy was added
to our union. My girl will be eight and my boy six years of age.

I made up my mind after I had the second child that in
spite of my health as I was hit by an auto while carrying the
first I would get some work to do but debts collected so rapidly
it almost took a derik to lift them let alone a sick woman.
I went to work evenings when my husband would be home
so as somebody could watch the baby and I did this until
the baby was three years old when I suggested taking in a man
who had been boarding with his sister as she moved to
Rochester and he had to look for a new place. Well my husband
agreed as he figured the $15 per he paid us would make it
easier for him as this man was a widower with two children
and as my husband knew him for twelve years being real pals
going out together etc. After the boarder was with us for
about a year my husband didn't come home one night and
then two nights etc. I listed him in the missing persons
and after two and a half months I was told to go to Grove St.
which I did and he was arrested on the charge of desertion
because he refused to support me and my kids. When he
served three months of the six the judge gave him he begged

me to give him another chance which like a fool I did and
when he got home he beat me up so I had to spend over $30
in the dentist afterwards.

He got a pension from the army and naturaly I was the one
to take it to the store and cash it as he was so lazy I always
had to sign his name and of course put per my name and
through wanting to pay the landlord because he wanted to put
us out I signed his check as usual but forgot to put per my
name and for this to get even with me because he did three
months time he sent to Washington for the copy of the check
so I could be arrested for forgery but as the butcher knew
about me signing the checks etc nothing was done to me.

He threatened my life many times saying no one solved
the Mrs. Mills murder and the same will happen to you and
many times when making beds I would find under his pillow
a hammer, scissors, knife, stone lifter etc and when I asked
him what the idea was he would make believe he knew
nothing about it or say the children put them there and then
a few months went by and I was going to my work as usual
as the boarder had to stay home that day due to the fact that
the material for his boss did not arrive which prevented him
from going to work as he is a piece worker. I always made
a habit of setting the breakfast table and preparing the food
the night before so I could stay in bed until seven as at that
time my son was in the Kings County hospital with a disease
which my husband gave me that he got while fighting for
Uncle Sam and I had to be at the clinic for the needle to.
So while I was in bed unbeknown to me my husband sent
the boarder out for a paper and when he came back my husband
was gone. So later when I came from my room I was told that
my husband had gone out. I fixed the childs breakfast and ate my
own then went to the washtub to do the weeks wash and
while the boarder was reading the paper at twelve o'clock noon
my mother came over to mind the baby for the afternoon as

I had a chance to go out and make a little money doing
house work. Things were a little out of order beds not dressed
and articles out of place and a little sweeping had to be done
as I was washing all morning and I did not have a chance
to do it so I thought I'd do it then while my mother was in
the house with her to help me so that I could finish quickly.
Hurrying at break neck speed to get finished I swept through
the rooms to make sure everything was spick and span so
when my husband came home he couldn't have anything to say.
We had three beds and I was on the last which was a double
bed when stooping to put the broom under the bed to get at the
lint and the dust when lo and behold I saw a face like the
mask of a devil with only the whites of the eyes showing
and hands clenched to choke anyone and then I saw it move
and I was so frighted that almost till night time I was histerical
and I was paralized from my waist down. I thought I would
never be able to walk again. A doctor was called for me by
my mother and he said the man ought to be put away to do a
thing like that. It was my husband lieing under the bed
from seven in the morning until almost half past one o'clock
lieing in his own dirt instead of going to the bath room
when he had to he dirtied himself waiting to frighten me.

So as I could not trust him I would not sleep with him
and as I told the boarder to find a new place because I thought
maybe he was jealous of something I slept in the boarders
bed in an other room. Some nights I would wake up and find
him standing by my bed laughing like a crazy man or
walking around stripped etc.

I bought a new sowing machine as I do some sowing for
other people to make both ends meet and one night while
I was out delivering my work I got back to find the house
cleaned out and he had pawned my sowing machine and also
all the other pawnables in the house. Ever since he frightened me

I have been so nervous during the night when I get up for
the children he would be standing behind a curtain and
either jump out at me or put his hand on me before I could
light the light. Well as I had to see that I could not make him
work steady and that I had to be mother and housekeeper
and wage earner etc and I could not let my nerves get the best
of me as I lost a good job once on account of having bad
nerves I simply moved away from him and anyway there was
nothing much left in the house. But he pleaded with me
for another chance so I thought seeing as he is the father of
my children I will and then he did more crazy things to numerous
to mention and I left him again. Four times we got together
and four times I left. Please Miss Lonelyhearts believe me
just for the childrens sake is the bunk and pardon me because
I dont know what sircumstances are but I know from experience that in over three years I got $200 from him
altogether.

About four months ago I handed him a warrant for his
arrest for non support and he tore it up and left the house
and I havent seen him since and as I had newmonia and my
little girl had the flu I was put in financial embarasment
with the doctor and we had to go to the ward and when we
came out of the hospital I had to ask the boarder to come
to live with us again as he was a sure $15 a week and if
anything happened to me he would be there to take care of the
children. But he tries to make me be bad and as there is
nobody in the house when he comes home drunk on Saturday
night I dont know what to do but so far I didnt let him.
Where my husband is I dont know but I received a vile letter
from him where he even accused his inocent children of things
and sarcasticaley asked about the star boarder.

Dear Miss Lonelyhearts please dont be angry at me for
writing such a long letter and taking up so much of your

142

precisious time in reading it but if I ever write all the things
which happened to me living with him it would fill a book
and please forgive me for saying some nasty things as I had to
give you an idea of what is going on in my home. Every woman
is intitled to a home isnt she? So Miss Lonelyhearts please
put a few lines in your column when you refer to this letter
so as I will know you are helping me. Shall I take my husband
back? How can I support my children?

Thank you for anything you can advise me in I remain
your truly

Broad-shoulders

P.S. Dear Miss Lonelyhearts dont think I am broad shouldered
but that is the way I feel about life and me I mean.

*

It was Broad-shoulders, Broken-hearted, Unfortunate-cripple,
Disillusioned-with-tubercular-husband and my many other
communicants who finally drove me to Christ. But don't
misunderstand me. My Christ has nothing to do with love.

Even before I became Miss Lonelyhearts, my world was
moribund. I lived on a deserted stairway, among steel
engravings of ornate machinery. I wrote my first love letters
on a typewriter. When I opened a door, I was a criminal
returning to the scene of his crime or a famous inventor
revisiting the humble shack of his birth.

The joke of suffering and the joke of comforting killed
this world. The stairway flattened into a desert, and when
I opened a letter addressed to Miss Lonelyhearts, two stones
touched.

I turned to Christ as the most familiar and natural of
excitants. I wanted him to destroy this hypnosis. He alone
could make the rock of sensation bleed and the stick of
thought flower.

While sitting in my room, working at this Christ business,
I became frightened and decided to go to Delehanty's speakeasy
for a drink. As I lifted my glass, Shrike, the feature editor,
caught my arm. "Ah, Miss Lonelyhearts," he said, "brooding
again, eh? You're morbid, my young friend, morbid."

Shrike practiced a trick used much by moving picture
comedians—the dead pan. No matter how fantastic or elaborate
his speech, he never changed his expression. Under the
shining white globe of his brow, his features huddled together
in a grey triangle.

He lifted his glass with a flourish. "I give you the renaissance,"
he shouted. "Forget the crucifixion, remember the renaissance.
There were no brooders then. What a period! What pageantry!
Drunken popes . . . Beautiful courtezans . . . Illegitimate
children . . ."

How had he discovered my preoccupation? I don't know.
But I felt sure it wasn't an accident. If I had been thinking
of the South Seas, he would have said, "Like Gauguin, eh?"

After some pantomine suggesting colorful pageantry,
he began again: " 'Brown Greek manuscripts and mistresses
with great smooth marbly limbs . . .' But that reminds me,
I'm expecting one of my admirers—a cow-eyed girl of great
intelligence." He illustrated the word intelligence by
carving two enormous breasts in the air. "She works in a
bookstore, but wait until you see her behind."

I made the mistake of showing my annoyance.

"So you don't care for women. J. C. is your only sweetheart,
eh? the King of Kings, the Miss Lonelyhearts of Miss
Lonelyhearts. . ."

At this moment, a young woman came up to the bar and
Shrike turned on her. She had long legs, thick ankles, big hands,
a powerful body, a slender neck and a childish face made
tiny by a man's haircut.

"Miss Farkis," he said, making her bow as a ventriloquist does his doll, "Miss Farkis, I want you to meet Miss Lonely-hearts. Show him, please, the same respect you show me. He too is a comforter of the poor in spirit, and a lover of God."

She acknowledged the introduction with a masculine handshake.

"Miss Farkis," Shrike said to me, "Miss Farkis works in a bookstore and writes on the side." He patted her rump.

"What were you talking about?" she asked.

"Religion."

"Get me a drink, and please continue. I'm very much interested in the new thomistic synthesis."

"St. Thomas!" Shrike shouted, as though terribly insulted. "What do you take us for, stinking intellectuals? We're not fake Europeans. We were discussing Christ, the Miss Lonelyhearts of Miss Lonelyhearts. America has her own religions, and, if you need a synthesis, here is the material for it." He took a clipping from his wallet and slapped it on the bar.

"ADDING MACHINE USED IN RITUAL OF WESTERN SECT . . . *Figures Will Be Used for Prayers for Condemned Slayer of Aged Recluse* . . . DENVER, COL., April 2 (A. P.) Frank H. Rice, Supreme Pontiff of the Liberal Church of America, has announced he will carry out his plans for a 'goat and adding machine' ritual for William Moya, condemned slayer, despite objection to his program by a Cardinal of the sect. Rice declared the goat would be used as part of a 'sackcloth and ashes' service shortly before and after Moya's execution, set for the week of June 20. Prayers for the condemned man's soul will be offered on an adding machine. Numbers, he explained, constitute the only universal language. Moya killed Joseph Zemp, an aged recluse, in an argument over a small amount of money."

Miss Farkis laughed and Shrike looked as though he were
going to punch her. His actions shocked the bartender who
hurriedly asked us to go into the back room. I didn't want to go
with them, but they insisted and I was too tired to argue.
We seated ourselves at a table inside one of the booths.
Shrike again raised his fist, but when she drew back he slipped
his hand inside the neck of her dress. The trick worked.
She gave in to his hand until he became too daring,
then pushed him away.

"I am a great saint," he shouted. "I can walk on my own
water. Haven't you ever heard of Shrike's Passion in the
Luncheonette, or the Agony in the Soda Fountain? Then I
compared the wounds in Christ's body to the mouths of a
miraculous purse in which we deposit the small change of our
sins. It is indeed an excellent conceit. But now let us consider
the holes in our own bodies, and into what these congenital
wounds open. Under the skin of a man is a wonderous
jungle where veins like lush tropical growths hang along
over-ripe organs and weed-like entrails writhe in squirming
tangles of red and yellow. In this jungle, flitting from rock-grey
lungs to golden intestine, from liver to lights and back to liver
again, lives a bird called the soul. The Catholic hunts this
bird with bread and wine, the Hebrew with a golden ruler,
the Protestant on leaden feet with leaden words, the Buddhist
with a string of beads, the Negro with blood. I spit on them all.
Phooh! And I call upon you to spit. Phooh! Do you stuff birds?
That's the question. Do you stuff birds? No, my dears,
taxidermy is not religion. No! A thousand times no.
Better, I say unto you, better a live bird in the jungle of the
body then two stuffed birds on the library table."

His caresses kept pace with the sermon, and when he

146

reached the end, he buried his thin grey face like the blade of a hatchet in her neck.

Contact
Vol. I, pp. 13-21
May 1932

Miss Lonelyhearts and the Clean Old Man

I went around to Delehanty's for a drink. A group of my friends were standing at the bar. They greeted me, and continued talking. As usual, the topic was literature. They were complaining about the number of female writers.

"And they've all got three names. Mary Roberts Wilcox, Ella Wheeler Cather, Ford Mary Rinehardt." . . .

Someone suggested raping them. That started a train of stories.

"I knew a gal who was regular until she fell in with a group and went literary. She began writing for the little magazines about how much Beauty hurt her and ditched her boy friend who set up pins in a bowling alley. The guys on the block got sore and took her into the lots one night. About eight of them. They ganged her proper." . . .

"That's like the one they tell about a female book-reviewer. When this hardboiled stuff first came in, she dropped the trick elocution and went in for scram and lam. She got to hanging around with a lot of mugs in a speak, gathering material for a novel. Well, the mugs didn't know they were picturesque and thought she was regular until the bartender put them wise. They got her into the back room to teach her a new word and put the boots to her. They didn't let her out for three days. On the third day they sold tickets to niggers. But here's the pay off—she finished the novel." . . .

I stopped listening. They would go on in this way until they were too drunk to talk. They were aware of their child-ishness, but did not know how else to revenge themselves. At college, and perhaps a year afterwards, they believed in literature, had believed in personal expression as a literary end. When they lost this belief, they lost everything. Money and fame meant nothing to them. They were not worldly men.

I drank steadily. Not until I heard my own name mentioned did I again begin to listen.

"He's a leper-licker. Shrike says he wants to lick lepers. Barkeep, a leper for the gent."

"Well, that's the trouble with his approach to God. It's too damn literary—plain song, Latin poetry, medieval painting, Huysmans, stained glass windows and crap like that."

"Even if he were to have a genuine religious experience, it would be personal and so meaningless, except to a psychologist."

"The trouble with him, the trouble with all of us, is that we have no outer life, only an inner one, and that by necessity."

"He's an escapist. He wants to cultivate his interior garden. But you can't escape into the past, and where is he going to find a market for the fruits of his personality. The Farm Board is a failure."

"What I say is, after all one has to earn a living. We can't all believe in Christ, and what does the farmer care about art. He takes his shoes off to get the warm feel of the rich earth between his toes. You can't take your shoes off at a concert or in a church."

"You guys are wrong, our young friend's homage to Christ, Man of Sorrows, wears a garb of understanding that lies too deep for tears. It does him proud. What matter if his daily column does not always subscribe to grammar's nice autocracy.

His is a brave transcending, and conveys so much that might
otherwise have gone unuttered." . . .

Was this nonsense the only barrier? Had I been thwarted
by such a low hurdle?

I felt warm and sure. Through the light blue tobacco
smoke the mahogany bar shone like wet gold, and the glasses
and bottles with their exploding highlights sounded like a
battery of little bells when they are touched together by the
bartender. I consciously lost myself in an evening long past.
My sister and I were waiting for father to come home from the
church. She was eight years old and I was twelve. I went to
the piano and began to play a dance piece by Mozart. I
had never voluntarily gone to the piano before. My sister began
to dance. She had never danced before. She danced gravely
and carefully, a simple dance yet formal . . . I thought of
children dancing. Square replacing oblong and being replaced
by circle. Every child, everywhere; in the whole world there was
not one child who was not gravely, sweetly dancing.

Backing away from the bar, I collided with a man holding
a glass of whiskey. I turned to beg his pardon and received
a blow in the mouth. Later I found myself at a table in the
backroom, playing with a loose tooth. I wondered why my hat
didn't fit, and discovered a lump on the back of my head.
I must have fallen. The hurdle was higher than I had thought.

My anger swung in large drunken circles. What in Christ's
name was this Christ business? And children gravely dancing?
I would ask to be transferred to the sports department.

Ned Gates came in to see how I was getting along and
suggested the open air. He also was very drunk. It had started
to snow. The snow was heavy and wet, and my anger grew
cold and sodden like the snow. We staggered along, turning
corners at random, until we found ourselves in front of the park.
A light was burning in the comfort station. We went in to
warm up.

An old man was sitting on one of the toilets. The door of
the stall was propped open, and he was sitting on the
turned-down toilet cover.

Gates hailed him. "Well, well, smug as a bug in a rug, eh?"

The old man jumped with fright. He finally managed to
speak. "What do you want? Please leave me alone." His voice
was like a flute; it did not vibrate.

"If you can't get a woman, get a clean old man," Gates sang.

The old man looked as if he were going to cry, but suddenly
laughed instead. A terrible cough started under his laugh,
and catching at the bottom of his lungs, it ripped into his
mouth. He turned away to wipe himself with some paper
from the roll beside the seat.

I tried to get Gates to leave, but he wouldn't go without
the old man. We grabbed him, and pulled him out of the booth
and through the door of the comfort station. He went soft
in my arms and started to giggle. I had to fight off the desire
to hit him.

The snow had stopped falling, and it had grown very cold.
The old man did not have an overcoat, but said that he
found the cold exhilarating. He evidently considered himself
an eccentric gentleman of the old school. He carried a cane
and wore gloves because they were dressy and because he
detested red hands.

Instead of going to Delehanty's, we went to an Italian cellar
close by the park. The old man tried to get us to drink
coffee, but we told him to mind his own business and drank
whiskey. His elaborate manners made us both sore.

"Listen, you," Gates said, "cut out the gentlemanly stuff,
and tell us the story of your life."

The old man drew himself up like a little girl making a
muscle.

"Aw, come off," Gates said. "We're scientists. He's Havelock Ellis and I'm Krafft-Ebing. When did you first discover homosexualist tendencies in yourself?"

"But I do like women, Mr. Ebing. When I was younger, I . . ."

"Yeh, I know, but how about your difference from other men?"

"How dare you. . ." He gave a little scream of indignation.

"Now, now," I said. "He didn't mean to insult you. Scientists have terrible manners. . . But you are a pervert, aren't you?"

He raised his cane to strike me. Gates grabbed it and wrenched it out of his hand. He began to cough violently, and having no handkerchief, held his black satin tie to his mouth. Still coughing, he dragged himself to a table in the back of the room.

I felt as I had felt years before when I had accidentally stepped on a frog. Its spilled guts filled me with pity, but my pity turned to rage when its suffering became real to my senses, and I beat it frantically until it was dead.

"I'll get the old bastard's life story," I shouted. "The lousy old stinker." Gates followed me laughing.

At our approach, the old man jumped to his feet. I caught him and forced him back into his chair.

"We're psychologists," I said. "We want to help you. What's your name?"

"George B. Simpson."

"What does the B stand for?"

"Bramhall."

"Your age and the nature of your quest?"

"By what right do you ask?"

"Science gives me the right."

"Let's drop it," Gates said. "The old fag is going to cry."

"No, Krafft-Ebing, sentiment must never be permitted to interfere with the probings of science."

I put my arm around the old man. "Tell us the story of your life," I said, loading my voice with sympathy. "We promise not to laugh."

"I have no story."

"You must have. Everyone has a life story."

The old man began to sob.

"Yes, I know," I said, "your tale is a sad one. Tell it."

When he still refused to speak, I took his arm and twisted it. Gates tried to tear me away, but I refused to let go. I was twisting the arm of all the sick and miserable, the broken and betrayed, the inarticulate and impotent.

The old man began to scream. Somebody hit me from behind with a chair.

Contact
Vol. 2, pp. 22-27
May 1932

Miss Lonelyhearts in the Dismal Swamp

*The Miss Lonelyhearts of the New York Evening Hawk
(Are you in trouble? Do you need advice? Write to
Miss Lonelyhearts and she will help you) sits staring through
his office window into the street. Piled on his desk are
letters from Broad-shouldered, Broken-hearted, Disillusioned-
with-tubercular-husband. Although the street is walled at
both ends, he has a Bible in one hand and a philosophy book
in the other. In his lap are travel, art, seed and gun catalogues.*

"Ah, Tahiti . . . Like Gauguin, eh? To dream away the days on the golden sand while the sun comes up like a red pool ball across the lagoon and the rhythm of a primitive

world enters your soul and you build a thatch hut and take
the daughter of a chief for a bride a slim young maiden with an
ancient wisdom in her eyes whose simple laughter charms
you with breasts like golden speckled pears and kisses like
rotten oranges and bananas and clotted cream the jungle
writhes up to your very door colored like a drawing in an
anatomy book while under the golden moon on the blue lagoon
you croon and soon as a boon you ask in the soft sylabelew
and vocabelew of her langorour tongue that you are no longer
white but golden brown so passing tourists have need of
an indignant finger but they envy you your breech clout and
carefree laugh and fingers instead of forks and little brown
bride so when a beautiful society girl under cover of darkness
comes to your hut you send her back to the yacht that hangs
on the horizon like a nervous racehorse and when the old king
dies you are king and rule gently but firmly over your beautiful
people while your white beard hangs like a nervous racehorse
on your barrel-like chest and when the god of death calls
you enter the jungle to die and where you fall the orchids
bloom langrosely red and the grass where buried Caesars bled
a richer green and a richer head.

"Or why not a farm, like Tolstoy? The ways and means
of men as getting and lending you lay waste your world is too
much with us and the bus takes too long while the subway
is crowded so you walk behind the enormous millstones
of your horse's moist behind no collar or tie and plow the broad
swift acres as the red-handled plow turns up the rich black
soil while the wind carries the smell of pine across the fields
and the rhythm of an old old work enters your blood as you
sow and weep and chivy your kine not kin between the rows
with the heavy sexual step of Indians dancing and tread the
seed down into the female earth no dragon's teeth but
beans and greens.

"Or why not take the cash and let the credit and shooting
in Scotland and Palm Beech and London in the spring oh to be
there so you are a patron of the arts and flowers and keep
herds of whores and Philadelphia Jack O'Brien with his
chestweights then you give a last party and everybody is dressed
in black and the waiters are coons and the table is a coffin
and you eat caviar and blackberries and licorice candy and
drink black coffee and you make a speech it's in the bag from the
start ere the echoes of the starting gun die away headlong
for the tape we plunge in the red with too big a nut yet play
up play the game although flies in the milk as well as the amber
we know full well but seeing as its better to lie down with a
full dog than a dead lion even if the cards are cold and marked
for emphasis by the hand of fate and you are in a club that
won't stand squawks where they deal only one hand and you
must sit in so get a run for your money tank up grab what's
on the buffet and use the girls in the upstairs rooms but when
you throw box cars take it with a dead pan.

"Be an artist or a writer. Great art is forever and a day
and when you are hungry and cold warm yourself before the
flaming tints of Titian and nourish yourself with great
spiritual foods by listening to the noble periods of Bach the
harmonies of Brahms and the music of Beethoven do you think
there is anything in the fact that their names all begin with B
but don't take a chance smoke a three B pipe and remember
those immortal lines when the remembrance of melody
the echo parting fails the falling day what a rhythm so tell
them to keep their society whores and pressed duck with oranges
but give you l'art vivant the living art as you call it and yes
tell them that you know your shoes are broken and there are
pimples on your face and you have buck teeth and a club foot
but that home you have a copy of The Brothers Karamazov
and tomorrow they are playing Beethoven's last quartets in
Carnegie Hall."

154

Politics, drugs, suicide, golf . . . no, the street is walled at both ends. Ah, Miss Lonelyhearts your soul is sick. Even when your team is winning you refuse to cheer. Salt, that's your trouble. You take everything with a grain of salt, forgetting that salt is the enemy of fire as well as of ice. Be warned, the salt you use is not Attic salt, it's coarse, butcher's salt. It doesn't preserve, it kills.

You're not one of those who swallow camels and strain at stools. Then my church is your only hope. The First Church of Christ Dentist. In the name of the Father, Son and Wire-haired Fox Terrier—the trinity new-style. To hell with St. Thomas Aquinas and the stinking intellectuals. Write J. C. a letter.

Dear Miss Lonelyhearts of
Miss Lonelyhearts:

I am twenty years old and in the newspaper game. Life for me is a desert empty of all comfort. I cannot find pleasure in food, drink, or women—nor do the arts give me joy any longer. The Leopard of Discontent walks the streets of my city; the Lion of Discouragement crouches outside the walls of my citadel. All is desolation and a vexation of the spirit. I feel like hell. How can I believe, how can I have faith in this day and age? Is it true that the greatest scientists believe again in you?

I read your column and like it very much. There you once wrote: "When the salt has lost its savour who shall savour it again?" Is the answer: "None but the saviour?"

Thanking you very much for a quick reply, I remain yours truly,

A Regular Subscriber.

Contempo
Vol. 2, pp. 1, 2
5 July 1932

Miss Lonelyhearts on a Field Trip

It was cold and damp in the city room the next day, and
Miss Lonelyhearts sat at his desk with his hands in his pockets
and his legs pressed together. He sat staring at a pile of letters.
A desert, he was thinking, not of sand, but of rust and body
dirt, surrounded by a backyard fence on which are posters
describing the events of the day. Mother slays five with ax,
slays seven, slays nine . . . Babe slams two, slams three . . . Inside
the fence Desperate, Broken-hearted, Dis-illusioned-with-
tubercular-husband and the rest were gravely building the
letters MISS LONELYHEARTS out of white-washed
clam shells.

He failed to notice Goldsmith's waddling approach until
his heavy arm dropped on his neck like the arm of a deadfall.
He freed himself with a grunt. His anger amused Goldsmith,
who smiled, bunching his fat cheeks like twin rolls of
smooth, pink toilet paper.

"Well, how's the drunkard?" Goldsmith asked.

Miss Lonelyhearts knew that Goldsmith had written his
column for him yesterday, so he hid his annoyance
to be grateful.

"No trouble at all," Goldsmith said, "It was a pleasure
to read your mail." He took a pink envelope out of his pocket
and threw it on the desk. "From an admirer." He winked,
letting a thick, grey lid down slowly and luxuriously over
a moist, rolling eye.

Miss Lonelyhearts picked up the letter.

Dear Miss Lonelyhearts—

I am not very good at writing so I wonder if I could have a
talk with you. I am only 32 years old but have had a lot of
trouble in my life and am unhappily married to a cripple.
I need some good advice bad but cant state my case in a letter

as I am not good at letters and it would take an expert
to state my case. I know your a man and am glad as I dont
trust women. You are pointed out to me in Delehanty's
as the man who does the advice in the paper and the minute
I saw you I said you can help me. You had on a blue suit and a
grey hat when I came in with my husband who is a cripple.

I dont feel to bad about asking to see you personal because
I feel almost like I knew you. So please call me up at
Burgess 7-7323 which is my number as I need your advice
bad about my married life.

An admirer

Fay Doyle

When Miss Lonelyhearts threw the letter into the wastepaper
basket with a great show of distaste, Goldsmith laughed at
him. "How now, Dostoevski?" he said, "that's no way to act.
Instead of pulling the Russian by recommending suicide,
you ought to get the lady with child and increase the potential
circulation of the paper."

To drive him away, Miss Lonelyhearts made believe that he
was busy. He bent over his typewriter and started pounding
out his column.

"Life, for most of us, seems a terrible struggle full of pain
and heartbreak, without hope or joy. But, oh, my dear readers,
it only seems so. Everyman, no matter how poor or humble,
can teach himself to use his senses. See the cloud-flecked sky,
the foam-decked sea . . . Smell the sweet pine and heady
privet . . . Feel of velvet and of satin . . . As the popular song
goes, 'The best things in life are free.' Life is . . . ."

When Goldsmith had gone, he turned again to the imagined
desert where Desperate, Broken-hearted and the others were
still building his name. They had run out of sea shells and
were using faded photographs, soiled fans, time tables,
playing cards, broken toys, imitation jewelry; junk that had

been made precious by memory, far more precious than anything
the sea might yield.

He killed his great understanding heart by laughing, and
reached into the wastepaper basket for Mrs Doyle's letter [.]
Like a pink tent, he set it over the desert. Against the dark
mahogany desk top, the cheap paper took on rich flesh tones.
He thought of Mrs Doyle as a tent, hair-covered and veined,
and of himself as the skeleton in the water closet, the skull
and cross bones on a scholar's bookplate. When he made the
skeleton enter the flesh tent, it flowered at every joint.

But despite the thoughts, he remained as dry and cold as a
polished bone, and sat trying to discover a moral reason for
not calling Mrs Doyle. If he could only believe in Christ,
then adultery would be a sin, then everything would be simple
and the letters extremely easy to answer.

The completeness of his failure drove him to the telephone.
He left the city room and went into the hall to use the pay
station from which all private calls had to be made. The walls
of the booth were covered with obscene drawings. He fastened
his eyes on two disembodied genitals copulating and gave
the operator Burgess 7-7323.

"Is Mrs Doyle in?"

"Hello, who is it?"

"I want to speak to Mrs Doyle," he said. "Is this Mrs Doyle?"

"Yes, that's me." Her voice was hard with fright.

"This is Miss Lonelyhearts."

"Miss who?"

"Miss Lonelyhearts, Miss Lonelyhearts, the man who
does the column."

He was about to hang up, when she cooed,

"Oh hello . . ."

"You said I should call."

"Oh, yes . . . what?"

He guessed that she wanted him to do the talking. "When can you see me?"

"Now." She was still cooing, and he could almost feel her warm, moisture laden breath through the ear-piece.

"Where?"

"You say."

"I'll tell you what," he said, "meet me in the park, near the obelisk, in about an hour."

He went back to his desk and finished his column, then started for the park. When he arrived at the obelisk, he sat down on a bench to wait for Mrs Doyle. Still thinking of tents, he examined the sky and saw that it was canvas-colored and ill-stretched. He examined it like a stupid detective who is searching for a clue to his own exhaustion. When he found nothing, he turned his trained eye on the skyscrapers that menaced the little park from all sides. In their tons of forced rock and tortured steel, he discovered what he thought was a clue.

Americans have dissipated their racial energy in an orgy of stone breaking. In their few years they have broken more stones than did centuries of Egyptians. And they have done their work hysterically, desperately, almost as if they knew that the stones would some day break them.

The detective saw a big woman enter the park and start in his direction. He made a quick catalogue: legs like Indian clubs, breasts like ballo[o]ns and a forehead like a pigeon. Despite her short plaid skirt, red sweater, rabbit skin jacket and knitted tam-o-shanter, she looked like a police captain.

He waited for her to speak first.

"Miss Lonelyhearts? Oh, hello . . ."

"Mrs Doyle?" He stood up and took her arm. It felt like a thigh.

"Where are we going?" she asked, as he began to lead her off.
"For a drink."

"I can't go to Delehanty's. They know me."

"We'll go to my place."

"Ought I?"

He did not have to answer, for she was already on her way.
As he followed her up the stairs to his apartment, he watched the
action of her massive hams; they were like two enormous
grindstones.

He made some highballs and sat down beside her on the bed.

"You must know an awful lot about women from your job,"
she said with a sigh, putting her hand on his knee.

He had always been the pursuer, but now found a strange
pleasure in having the roles reversed. He drew back when
she reached for a kiss. She caught his head and put her tongue
into his mouth. At first it ticked like a watch, then the tick
softened and thickened into a heart throb. It beat louder and
more rapidly each second, until he thought that it was going
to explode, and pulled away with a rude jerk.

"Don't," she begged.

"Don't what?"

"Oh, darling, turn out the light."

He smoked a cigarette, standing in the dark and listening
to her undress. She made sea sounds: something flapped
like a sail, there was the creak of ropes, then he heard the
wave-against-a-wharf smack of rubber on flesh. Her call for
him to hurry was a sea-moan, and when he lay beside her,
she heaved, tidal, moon-driven.

Some fifteen minutes later, he crawled out of bed like an
exhausted swimmer leaving the surf, and dropped down in a
large armchair near the window. She went into the bathroom,
then came back and sat in his lap.

"I'm ashamed of myself," she said. "You must think I'm a bad woman."

He shook his head no.

"My husband isn't much. He's a cripple like I wrote you, and much older than me." She laughed. "He's all dried up. He hasn't been a husband to me for years. You know, Mary, my kid, isn't his."

He saw that she expected him to be astonished and did his best to lift his eyebrows.

"It's a long story," she said. "It was on account of Mary that I had to marry him. I'll bet you must have wondered how it was I came to marry a cripple. It's a long story."

Her voice was as hypnotic as a tom-tom, and as monotonous. Already his mind and body were half asleep.

"It's a long, long story, and that's why I couldn't write it in a letter. I got into trouble when the Doyle's lived above us on Center Street. I used to be kind to him and go to the movies with him because he was a cripple although I was one of the most popular girls on the block. So when I got into trouble I didn't know what to do and asked him for money for an abortion. But he didn't have the money, so we got married instead. It all came through my trusting a dirty dago. I thought he was a gent but when I asked him to marry me, why he spurned me from the door and wouldn't even give me money for an abortion. He said if he gave me the money that would mean it was his fault and I would have something in him. Did you ever hear of such a skunk?"

"No," he said. The life out of which she spoke was even heavier than her body. It was as if a gigantic, living Miss Lonelyhearts letter in the shape of a paper weight had been placed on his brain.

"After the baby was born, I wrote the skunk, but he never wrote back, and about two years ago I got to thinking how unfair it was for Mary to have to depend on a cripple and not

to come into her rights. So I looked his name up in the telephone
book and took Mary to see him. As I told him then, not that
I wanted anything for myself, but just that I wanted Mary
to get what was coming to her. Well, after keeping us waiting
in the hall over an hour—I was boiling mad, I can tell you,
thinking of the wrong he had done me and my child—we were
taken into the parlor by the butler. Very quiet and lady-like,
because money aint everything and he's no more a gent than
I'm a lady, the dirty wop—I told him he ought to do something
for Mary see'n he's her father. Well, he had the nerve to say
that he had never seen me before and that if I didn't stop
bothering him, he'd have me run in. That got me riled and
I lit into the bastard and gave him a piece of my mind.
A woman came in while we were arguing that I figured was
his wife, so I hollered, 'He's the father of my child, he's the
father of my child!' When they went to the phone to call a
cop, I picked up the kid and beat it. And now comes the
funniest part of the whole thing. Martin my husband, is a
queer guy and he always makes believe that he is the father
of the kid and even talks to me about *our* child. Well, when
we got home, Mary kept asking me why I said a strange
man was her poppa. She wanted to know if Martin wasn't
really her poppa. I must have been crazy because I told her
that she should remember that her poppa was a man named
Tony Benelli and that he had wronged me. I told her a lot of
other crap like that—too much movies I guess. Well, when
Doyle got home the first thing Mary says to him is that he
aint her poppa. That got him sore and he wanted to know
what I had told her. I didn't like his high falutin' ways and said,
'The truth!' I guess too that I was kind a sick of see'n him
moon over her. He went for me and hit me on the cheek.
I wouldn't let no man get away with that so I socked him back
and he swung at me with his stick but missed and fell on the

floor and started to cry. The kid was on the floor crying too
and that set me off because the next thing I know I'm on the
floor bawling too."

She waited for him to comment, but he remained silent
until she nudged him into speech with her elbow. "Your
husband probably loves you and the kid," he said.

"Maybe so, but I was a pretty girl and could of had my pick.
What girl wants to spend her life with a shrimp of a
cripple."

"You're still pretty," he said because he was frightened.

She rewarded him with a kiss, then dragged him limping
to the bed.

Contact
Vol. 1, pp. 50-57
October 1932

Some Notes on Violence

Is there any meaning in the fact that almost every manuscript
we [at *Contact* magazine] receive has violence for its core?
They come to us from every state in the Union, from every
type of environment, yet their highest common denominator
is violence. It does not necessarily follow that such stories
are the easiest to write or that they are the first subjects
that young writers attempt. Did not sweetness and light
fill the manuscripts rejected, as well as accepted, by the
magazines before the [1914-1918] war, and Art those
immediately after it? We did not start with the ideas of
printing tales of violence. We now believe that we would be
doing violence by suppressing them.

— * —

In America violence is idiomatic. Read our newspapers.
To make the front page a murderer has to use his imagination,

he also has to use a particularly hideous instrument. Take
this morning's paper: FATHER CUTS SON'S THROAT IN
BASEBALL ARGUMENT. It appears on an inside page.
To make the first page, he should have killed three sons and
with a baseball bat instead of a knife. Only liberality and
symmetry could have made this daily occurence interesting.

— * —

And how must the American writer handle violence?
In the July [1932] "Criterion", H. S. D[ykes] says of a story
in our first number that ". . . the thing is incredible, as an event,
in spite [of] its careful detail, simply because such things
cannot happen without arousing the strongest emotions in
the spectator.["] Does not H. S. D. mean, "in the *breast* of the
spectator?") ["]Accordingly["] (the reviewer continues),
["]only an emotional description of the scene will be
credible . . ." Credible to an Englishman, yes, perhaps, or to a
European, but not to an American. In America violence is daily.
If an "emotional description" in the European sense is given an
act of violence, the American would say, "What's all the
excitement about," or, "By God, that's a mighty fine piece of
writing, that's art."

— * —

What is melodramatic in European writing is not necessarily
so in American writing. For a European writer to make
violence real, he has to do a great deal of careful psychology
and sociology. He often needs three hundred pages to motivate
one little murder. But not so the American writer. His audience
has been prepared and is neither surprised nor shocked if he
omits artistic excuses for familiar events. When he reads
a little book with eight or ten murders in it, he does not
necessarily condemn the book as melodramatic. He is far
from the ancient Greeks, and still further from those people

who need the naturalism of Zola or the realism of Flaubert
to make writing seem "artistical[l]y true."

Contact
Vol. 1, pp. 132-133
October 1932

Christmass Poem

The spread hand is a star with points
The fist a torch
Workers of the World
Ignite
Burn Jerusalem
Make of the City of Birth a star
Shaped like a daisy in color a rose
And bring
Not three but one king
The Hammer King to the Babe King
Where nailed to his six-branched tree
Upon the sideboard of a Jew
Marx
Performs the miracles of loaves and fishes

The spread hand is a star with points
The fist a torch
Workers of the World
Unite
Burn Jerusalem

Contempo
Vol. 3, p. 4
21 February 1933

Some Notes on Miss L.

I can't do a review of *Miss Lonelyhearts*, but here, at random,
are some of the things I thought when writing it:

As subtitle: "A novel in the form of a comic strip." The
chapters to be squares in which many things happen through
one action. The speeches contained in the conventional balloons.
I abandoned this idea, but retained some of the comic strip
technique: Each chapter instead of going forward in time,
also goes backward, forward, up and down in space like
a picture. Violent images are used to illustrate commonplace
events. Violent acts are left almost bald.

*   *   *

Lyric novels can be written according to Poe's definition
of a lyric poem. The short novel is a distinct form especially
fitted for use in this country. France, Spain, Italy have a
literature as well as the Scandinavian countries. For a hasty
people we are too patient with the Bucks, Dreisers and Lewises.
Thank God we are not all Scandinavians.

Forget the epic, the master work. In America fortunes do not
accumulate, the soil does not grow, families have no history.
Leave slow growth to the book reviewers, you only have
time to explode. Remember William Carlos Williams'
description of the pioneer women who shot their children
against the wilderness like cannonballs. Do the same
with your novels.

*   *   *

Psychology has nothing to do with reality nor should it be
used as motivation. The novelist is no longer a psychologist.
Psychology can become something much more important.
The great body of case histories can be used in the way the

ancient writers used their myths. Freud is your Bullfinch; you can not learn from him.

* * *

With this last idea in mind, Miss Lonelyhearts became the portrait of a priest of our time who has a religious experience. His case is classical and is built on all the cases in James' *Varieties of Religious Experience* and Starbuck's *Psychology of Religion.* The psychology is theirs not mine. The imagery is mine. Chapt. I—maladjustment. Chapt. III— the need for taking symbols literally is described through a dream in which a symbol is actually fleshed. Chapt. IV— deadness and disorder; see Lives of Bunyan and Tolstoy. Chapt. VI—self-torture by conscious sinning: see life of any saint. And so on.

* * *

I was serious therefore I could not be obscene.
I was honest therefore I could not be sordid.
A novelist can afford to be everything but dull.

Contempo
Vol. 3, pp. 1, 2
15 May 1933

Business Deal

For an hour after his barber left him, Mr. Eugene Klingspiel, West Coast head of Gargantual Pictures, worked ceaselessly. First he read *The Hollywood Reporter*, *Variety*, and *The Film Daily*. Then he measured out two spoonfuls of bicarbonate and lay down on the couch to make decisions. Before long Mr. Klingspiel had fallen into what he called a gentle reverie. He saw Gargantual Pictures swallowing its competitors like a boa-constrictor, engulfing whole amusement chains. In a delicious half-doze, he found himself wondering whether to absorb Balaban & Katz; but finding no use for Katz, he absorbed only Balaban, and turned next to Spyros Skouras and his seven brothers. Perhaps at the outset he ought to absorb only three of them. But which three? The three in the middle or two on one end and one on the other? Finally he arranged the eight Skourases into a squad of tin soldiers and executed five at random. The repeated buzz of the dictograph cut short his delicious sport. He flipped the switch irritably.

"Who is it?"

"Hwonh hwonh hwonh hwonh hwonh."

"I'll see them later," said Mr. Klingspiel. "Send in Charlie Baer."

"Hwonh-hwonh."

He lit a cigar, turned his back on the door, and set his features into a scowl which would have done credit to a Japanese print. No punk kid two years out of Columbia College could hold *him* up for money, no matter how many hit pictures he'd written. After a dignified interval, he swung around. Charlie Baer, moon-faced and unconcerned, was staring out of another window with his back to Mr. Klingspiel.

"Well, Charlie." Mr. Klingspiel controlled his irritation at this breach of respect and essayed a kindly smile. "I sent for you yesterday."

"Aha." Charlie stared placidly at Mr. Klingspiel. His dewy innocence was positively revolting.

"My girl phoned you at the Writers' Building, but they said you were working with Roy Zinsser in Malibu." Mr. Klingspiel cleared his throat. Maybe a good joke would clear the atmosphere. "Vas you dere, Sharlie?" He regretted it immediately; Charlie's frigid stare made his remark almost indelicate. So this weasel thinks he can hijack me, Mr. Klingspiel reflected angrily.

"Charlie," he began, screwing his face into an expression of deep disapproval, "I dint like that last script. It lacked guts. It dint have the most important thing a good comedy script should have."

"What's that?" asked Charlie without curiosity.

"Spontinuity," replied Mr. Klingspiel gravely. "Now if I were you, Charlie, I'd take that idea home and maul it around in your mind over-night."

"Oke," said Charlie, reaching for his hat.

"Oh, just one more thing." Mr. Klingspiel made believe he was consulting some papers. "You expire on the fifteenth, am I right?"

"Yep."

"Well, Charlie, I'm gonna lay it on the line. You did some great pictures. I'm gonna extend you another year, but this time at two-fifty a week." Charlie's eyes remained fixed on his. Mr. Klingspiel was radiant. "In other words, double what you're getting now. How's that?"

"No good," said Charlie. "Five hundred a week or I don't work."

"Listen to me," said Klingspiel. "Answer me one thing. How many fellers do you know twenty-three years old that make two-fifty a week?"

"I've got to think about my old age," said Charlie.

"When I was twenty-three," went on Mr. Klingspiel, well into his Plowboy-to-President mood, "what was I? A green kid working for buttons. All I could afford was a bowl of milk and crackers. You don't know how lucky you are."

"Yes, I do," said Charlie. "I once tried a bowl of milk and crackers."

"Now, look here, Charlie," said Mr. Klingspiel patiently, "why don't you get wise to yourself? A single man like you in no time could bank—"

"Five hundred," interrupted Charlie bovinely.

Mr. Klingspiel drummed softly on his desk.

"Listen, Charlie," he said after a moment, "let me tell you a story. It's a story about Adolph Rubens, the man who founded this great organization." Charlie's eyes drooped slightly. "Just picture to yourself that there ain't no Hollywood, no film business, nothing. It's twenty-eight years ago. A poor little furrier named Adolph Rubens is walking down a windy street in St. Louis. He's a little man, Charlie, but he's a fighter. He's cold and hungry, but in that man's brain is a dream. Everybody laughs at him and calls it Rubens' Folly, but he don't care. Why? Because in his brain he sees a picture of a mighty amusement ennaprise bringing entertainment and education to millions of people from coast to coast. And today that dream has come true. This ain't a business, Charlie; it's a monument created by the public to Adolph Rubens' ideals, and we're building all the time."

"Five hundred dollars or I stop building," said Charlie in the same metallic tone.

"Charlie," said Mr. Klingspiel after a moment, "I want you to do something. Come here. Not there—come around this side of the desk." He arose. "Now you sit down in my chair. That's right." He encircled the desk, then turned and faced Charlie. "Now put yourself in my place. You're Eugene Klingspiel, the head of Gargantual Pictures. You got a payroll of three hundred and forty-six thousand dollars a week. You got stars that are draining you dry. Nobody goes to pictures any more, they stay home and listen to the radio. You got a lot of dead-wood writers drawing their check like clockwork every Wednesday. Now, in walks a fella named Charlie Baer. He don't want much, only the shirt off your back. And what do you say to him?" He gripped the edges of the desk and stared into Charlie's face.

"Five hundred dollars or I turn in my badge," droned Charlie. Mr. Klingspiel's eyes glittered. The mongoose sat comfortably and waited for the cobra to strike again.

"Now let's be sensible," said Mr. Klingspiel. "I could buy four gagmen for what I'm paying you." Charles stood up. "But I'll tell you what I'm gonna do. Three hundred—"

"Mr. Klingspiel," said Charlie, "there's something I ought to tell you. Metro—"

"What?" Mr. Klingspiel quivered like a stag.

"Metro offered me four-fifty yesterday."

"So that's it," said Mr. Klingspiel. "That's how much loyalty you got. We pick you up from the gutter—four-twenty-five!"

"Listen," said Charlie coldly, "I'm a scenario-writer, not a peddler." He put on his hat.

"Just a minute," said Mr. Klingspiel. His face cleared suddenly. "I'm gonna teach that Metro crowd a lesson. Beginning the fifteenth Charlie Baer gets five hundred dollars a week from Gargantual—and Eugene Klingspiel *personally* guarantees that! And any time you got any problems I want you to come— Where you going?"

"Lunch," said Charlie, and smiled briefly. "You know, just a bowl of milk and crackers."

Mr. Klingspiel belched and grabbed for the bicarbonate.

Soft Soap for the Barber

Father Goose: The Story of Mack Sennett, by Gene Fowler.
New York: Covici, Friede. [1934.] 407 pages. $3.

From Shirtsleeves to Shirtsleeves in one generation is just
as true an American legend as from Ploughboy to President
or from Poland to Polo. Moreover, we, who are without
ambition, prefer it.

Mack Sennett went from boilermaker to president of the
Keystone Company. The Keystone Company is finished
and so is Mack Sennett. This fact should make everyone but
Gilbert Seldes feel a little better. Perhaps one day a final
chapter will be written to Drinkwater's biography of
Carl Laemmle and to Will Irwin's biography of Adolph Zukor.
Perhaps they too will go the way of Mack Sennett.
Hope springs eternal, etc.

And yet, maybe the men who make the pictures are not to
blame. Perhaps we should blame the man for whom the
pictures are made—"the barber in Peoria." As Fowler says,
"The history of the cinema indicates that a man will pay a
dollar to get a dime's worth of entertainment, but will not part
with a dime to get a dollar's worth of ideals"—or ideas.
Fowler is right. Whenever somebody forgets this fact, forgets
to ask what "the barber in Peoria" will think, a great deal
of money is lost.

It is strange, but the movies are always trying to forget
"the barber." Even Mack Sennett tried *once* to forget him.
He lost several hundred thousand dollars, then took another
look at the sign hanging on the wall of his scenario department.
"Remember: The extent of intelligence of the average public
mind is eleven years. Moving pictures should be made
accordingly." Sennett never forgot again.

Other Hollywood directors and supervisors never seem
to learn this lesson. Every year some one of them gets a
little punch-drunk, goes highbrow and forgets "the barber."
A picture like "The Crowd" is the result. "The barber" remains
in his barbershop and the theatres are empty. It takes two
or three films like "Dames" to get him to the Bijoux again.

Of course many things can be said in defense of "the barber."
Gene Fowler wisely leaves that to Gilbert Seldes; we prefer
to leave it to Mike Gold, and no offense meant.

The New Republic
Vol. 81, p. 23
14 November 1934

Bird and Bottle

Earle Haines stood in front of the saddlery store on Vine
Street, Hollywood. In the window of the store was an enormous
Mexican saddle covered with heavy silver ornaments. Around
the saddle was a collection of torture instruments: fancy,
braided quirts loaded with lead, spurs that had great, spiked
wheels; heavy, double bits that needed only a few pounds
pressure to dislocate the jaw of a horse. On a low shelf,
running across the back of the window, was a row of boots.
Some of them were black, others a pale yellow color. They all
had scalloped tops and very high heels.

Every day and all day, Earle stood in front of this store.
He stood stiffly, looked straight in front of him. His eyes never
followed the people who passed, but remained fixed on a
sign on the roof of the one-story building across the street.
The sign read: "Malted Milks—Too Thick for a Straw."
Regularly, twice every hour, Earle pulled a sack of tobacco

and a sheaf of papers from his shirt pocket and rolled a cigarette. Then he tightened the cloth of his trousers by lifting his knee and struck a match along the underside of his thigh.

He was a little under six feet tall. The big hat he wore added another eight inches to his height and the heels of his boots still another three. His pole-like appearance was exaggerated by the narrowness of his shoulders and his complete lack of either hips or buttocks. The years he had spent in saddle had made him bow-legged. In fact his legs were so straight that his dungarees, bleached a pale blue, hung down without a wrinkle. They hung as though empty. They were turned up at the bottom to form very wide cuffs and to show five inches of fancy boot. Over his left arm, neatly folded, was a dark grey jacket. His cotton shirt was navy blue with large white polka-dots, each one the size of a dime. The sleeves of his shirt were not rolled, but pulled up to the middle of his forearm and held there by a pair of rose-colored armbands.

Next to Earle was another young man. This one sat on his heels. He also wore a big hat and high-heeled boots. He, however, had on a suit of city clothes, cheap and over-styled with padded shoulders and high, pointed lapels. Close behind him was a battered paper valise that was held together by some heavy rope tied with professional-looking knots. Like Earle, he rarely moved his head, but his jaws champed continuously on a large wad of gum.

A third man sidled up to the store. He wore the same head and foot gear as the others. He spent a few minutes examining the merchandise in the window, then turned and looked across the street.

" 'Lo, boys," he said finally.

" 'Lo, Shoop," said the man next to Earle.

Shoop saw the paper valise and prodded it with the toe of his boot.

"Going someplace, Calvin?" he asked.

"Azusa," Calvin replied. "There's a rodeo."

"You going, Earle?"

"Nope," he said without turning his head. "I got a date."

Shoop considered this information for fully ten minutes before he spoke again.

"Columbia's making a new horse-opera," he said. "Ferris told me they'll use more than forty mounted-actors."

Calvin turned to Earle.

"Still got that fur vest?" he asked. "It'll cinch you a job as a sheriff."

This was a joke. Calvin and Shoop chuckled and slapped their thighs loudly. Earle paid no attention to them.

They liked to kid Earle, and tried to think of another joke.

"Ain't your old man still got some cows?" Calvin asked, winking at Shoop. "Why don't you go home?"

Shoop answered for Earle.

"He dassint. He got caught in a sheep car."

It was another joke, and a good one. Calvin and Shoop slapped their thig[h]s. After this they became silent and immobile again. About an hour later Calvin moved, then spoke.

"There goes your girl," he said.

Faye drove by the store and pulled into the curb some fifteen feet further on. Calvin and Shoop touched the brims of their hats, but Earle did not move. He was taking his time, as befitted his manly dignity. Not until she tooted her horn loudly did he begin to move. He walked toward the Ford touring car.

" 'Lo Honey," he said, taking off his hat.

"Hello, cowboy," Fay[e] said, looking at him with a smile.

She thought him very handsome. He was. He had the kind of two-dimensional face a talented child might draw with a ruler and compass. His chin was perfectly round and his large eyes were also round. His horizontal mouth ran at right angles to his long, perpendicular nose. The eveness of his complexion heightened his resemblance to a mechanical drawing. His face was the same color from hair-line to throat, as though the tan had been washed in by an expert.

"Get in," Faye said, opening the door of the Ford.

He put on his jacket, adjusting the collar and sleeves with great care, then climbed in beside her. She started the car with a jerk. When she got to Hollywood Boulevard she turned left. She was watching him out of the corner of her eye and saw that he was preparing to speak. She tried to hurry him.

"Get going, cowboy. What is it?"

"Look here, Honey. I ain't got no money for supper."

"Then we don't eat."

He considered this for a few minutes.

"Well, we got some grub at camp."

"Beans, I suppose."

"Nope."

She prodded him.

"Well, what are we going to eat?"

"Miguel and me's got some traps out."

Faye laughed angrily.

"Rat traps, huh? We're going to eat rats."

Earle laughed, but he did not say anything. She waited for him to speak, then pulled to the curb and slammed on the emergency brake. She was very sore.

"Listen, you big, strong, silent dope, either make sense or get out of this car."

"They're quail traps," he said apologetically.

She ignored his answer.

"Let me tell you something," she scolded—"talking to you is too damned much like work. You wear me out."

"I didn't mean nothing, Honey. I was only funning. I wouldn't feed you a rat."

She slammed off the brake and started the car. At Zacarias Street, she turned into the hills. After the car had climbed steadily for about half a mile she turned into a dirt road and followed that to its end.

Most of her anger had disappeared when she looked at him again. He was so handsome and had such a beautiful tan. She got out of the car.

"Give me a kiss," she said.

He took his hat off politely and wrapped his long arms around her. She noticed that he closed his eyes and puckered up his lips like a little boy. But there was nothing boyish about what he did to her. Both his hands and his lips were very active.

When she had had as much as she wanted, she shoved him away. Her hands went to her hair, then she took out a compact and fixed her face.

Faye was about seventeen years old and very pretty. She had wide straight shoulders, narrow hips and long legs. Under her tight sweater, her tiny breasts showed like the twin halves of a lemon. She had no hat on. Her "platinum" hair was drawn tightly away from her face and gathered together in back by a narrow baby blue ribbon that allowed it to tumble loosely on her shoulders. The style of her coiffure had been copied from Tennel's drawings of Alice.

Earle started along the little path that began where the dirt road ended. She followed him. They entered a canyon and began to climb.

It was Spring. Wherever weeds could find a purchase in the steep banks of the canyon they flowered in purple, blue

and pale pink. Orange poppies bordered the path. Their petals
were wrinkled like crepe and their leaves were heavy with
talcum-like dust.

They climbed still higher until they reached another canyon.
Here no flowers grew in the decomposed granite. But the
bare ground and the rocks were brilliantly colored. The earth
was silver with streaks of rose-gray and the rocks were turquoise
and lavender. Even the air was a vibrant pink.

They stopped to watch a humming bird chase a blue jay.
The jay flashed by squawking with its tiny enemy on its tail
like an emerald bullet. The gaudy birds seemed to burst the
colored air into a thousand glittering particles.

When they gained the top of the hill, they saw below them
a little green valley thick with trees. They made for it.
Miguel came to meet them at the edge of the wood.
He greeted Faye ceremoniously.

"Welcome, welcome, chinita."

The Mexican was short and heavily muscled. His skin was
the color of milk chocolate and [he] had Armenian eyes.
He wore a long-haired sweater—called a "gorilla" in and around
Los Angeles—with nothing under it. His white duck trousers
were badly soiled.

Faye followed the two men to their camp. There was a fire
burning between two rocks and she sat down next to it
on a broken swivel chair.

"When do we eat?" she demanded.

Miguel put a grill over the fire and started to scour a large
frying pan with sand. He gave Faye a knife and some
potatoes to peel.

Earle took up a burlap sack and moved off into the woods.
He followed a narrow cattle path until he came into a little
clearing covered with high, tufted grass. He stopped for a

moment behind a scrub oak to make sure that no one was
watching him.

A mocking bird sang in a nearby bush. Its song was like
pebbles being dropped one by one from a height into a pool
of water. Then a quail began to call, using two soft, almost
guttural notes. Another quail answered and the birds talked
back and forth. Their call was not like the cheerful whistle
of the Eastern bobwhite. It was full of melancholy and
weariness, yet marvelously sweet. Still another quail joined the
duet. This one called from near the center of the clearing.
It was a trapped bird, but the sound it made had no anxiety
in it, only sadness, impersonal and without hope.

Earle went to the trap, a wire basket about the size of a
washtub. When he stooped over, five birds ran wildly around
the inner edge and threw themselves against the chicken wire.
One of them, a cock, had a dainty plume on his head that
curled forward almost to his beak. Earle opened a little door
in the top of the trap and reached in. He caught the birds
one at a time and pulled their heads off before dropping
them into the sack.

He started back. As he walked along, he held the sack under
his left arm and plucked the birds. Their feathers fell to the
ground point first, weighed down by the tiny drops of blood
that trembled on the tips of their quills.

When Faye had finished the potatoes, she put them to soak
in a pan of water. The sun had gone down and it was chilly.
She huddled close to the fire. Miguel saw her shiver and
got out a jug of tequilla. They both drank deeply. Earle came
along just as they were having a second shot. He dropped
his sack and took the jug.

Miguel tried to show Faye how plump the birds were,
but she refused to look. He took them and washed them in a
pail of water, then began cutting them into quarters with a

pair of heavy tin shears. Faye tried not to hear the soft click the steel made as it cut through flesh and bone.

While the meal was cooking, while they ate and afterwards, they passed the jug. Faye grew hot and excited. She smoked a lot of cigarettes.

Both men stared at her. She knew what they were thinking but seemed not to care. She assumed enticing positions and made little, obscene gestures with her tongue and hands. Miguel opened his mouth several times as though to shout, but only gulped a deep breath of air. Earle shifted uneasily on his haunches and began to curse quietly.

Faye was frightened, but her fear, instead of making her wary, made her still more reckless. She took a long pull at the jug and got up to dance. She held her skirt well above her knees and did a slow rhumba. Her round bare thighs flashed silver and rose in the half-dark. She shook her yellow head.

Miguel made music for her. He clapped his hands and sang: "Tony's wife. . ."

Earle beat out the rhythm on a box with a thick stick.

"Tony's wife . . ."

Miguel stood up to dance. He struck the soft ground heavily with his feet and circled around her. They danced back to back and bumped each other.

Earle, too, began to dance. He did a crude hoe-down, the only dance he knew. He leaped into the air, knocked his heels together and whooped. But he felt out of it. Despite the noise he made, they ignored him.

The slow beat of the rhumba went on. Faye and the Mexican retreated and advanced, came together and separated again with a precision that only the blood knows.

She saw the blow before it fell. She saw Earle raise his stick and bring it down on Miguel's head. She heard the thud and saw him go to his knees still dancing, his body reluctant to acknowledge the interruption.

There is release in running; flight, too, is of the blood.
She ran up the hill, then down into the canyon, then down
into the next canyon.

She sat down on a fender. In a little while her breathing
became normal again and her heart stopped pounding. The
violent exercise had driven most of the heat out of her blood,
but there was still enough left to make her tingle pleasantly.
She felt comfortably relaxed, even happy.

Somewhere in the canyon a bird began to sing. She listened
to its song and sighed with pleasure. At first the low, rich
music sounded like water dripping on something hollow,
the bottom of a silver pot perhaps; then like a stick dragged
slowly over the strings of a harp.

The bird stopped as suddenly as it had begun. She got into
the Ford and drove off down the hill.

Pacific Weekly
Vol. 5, pp. 329-331
10 November 1936

Index

204

THE SERIF SERIES: BIBLIOGRAPHIES AND CHECKLISTS

GENERAL EDITOR: William White, Wayne State University
